A declaration of the joys of savoury baking. As exciting as any sweet baking book, it is filled with recipes you'll make time and time again. From bacon and egg breakfast buns to butter chicken pie, this was a book I devoured, from its beautiful design and imagery, to its modern, thoughtful recipes, and this is a book that should find a place in any baker's kitchen.

EDD KIMBER, baker, author, @theboywhobakes

Michael's book is both extraordinarily beautiful and inspiring, but more importantly, it is also comprehensive: with superb, easy-to-follow step-by-step instructions for utterly delicious recipes that you will actually bake, making it perfect for any level of baker.

VANESSA KIMBELL, The Sourdough School, author

I have been a massive fan of Michael James ever since I visited him at Tivoli Road Bakery where he was baking some of the best bread and pastries in Melbourne. We loved his first book, *The Tivoli Road Baker*, and it's always on the shelf in our kitchen and bakery.

His new book, *All Day Baking*, is savoury baking genius, with the chapters set out beautifully, and not surprisingly full of the most tempting and delicious recipes for the whole family. We can't wait to start baking from his book.

JUSTIN GELLATLY, baker, author, the doughnut guy

FOREWORD

Michael came to work with me first at Pied à Terre in London, back in the '90s, and that's where he met his lovely wife, Pippa, so I have known the two of them for almost twenty-five years. In this time, Michael has had a wealth of experience working in many establishments between the UK and Australia. He also worked with me in the very early days of my restaurant Tom's Kitchen, running the pastry and with me in the kitchen.

Sustainable suppliers were at the heart of our beliefs at Tom's Kitchen, and these values are now an integral part of Michael's life too. Michael believes in supporting local farmers who are using sustainable agricultural methods and who work with nature for the best results.

He was a chef first who then chose baking; with Pippa he founded The Tivoli Road Bakery in Melbourne in 2013. His amazing first book *The Tivoli Road Baker* was released in 2017, and in it he shares his own detailed thoughts on bread, particularly the art of sourdough, but also his love of ingredients generally.

Through his commitment, drive and ambition, he has grown to be one of the best regarded bakers in Australia. This book, *All Day Baking*, is a testament to his magnificent skills as a chef and his depth of knowledge and understanding of specialist and household ingredients.

Having a book like this in your kitchen will not only improve your cooking skills, but it will lighten your workload and encourage you to think and plan and reap the rewards. Every recipe is designed for everyday use and not just special occasions – I suggest some of you will want to try each recipe, page by page.

Whether it brings some much-needed order in a time of rush-rush and chaos, or helps you deliver a dinner party treat, quick snack, or something to spoil your kids, whether it explains that little niggling pastry method that you never had the time to master – it's all here in the most perfect of cookbooks, for the novice or beginner, the home cook that wants to go to the next level. Definitely your new go-to.

TOM AIKENS

ALL DAY BAKING

SAVOURY, NOT SWEET

PIES, QUICHES, GALETTES, TARTS, PRESERVES AND MORE

ALL DAY BAKING

SAVOURY, NOT SWEET

PIES, QUICHES, GALETTES, TARTS, PRESERVES AND MORE

Michael James
with Pippa James

Hardie Grant

BOOKS

Dedicated to Clover. Thank you for being the most honest critic, and for helping to shape this book. We love you.

In memory of Gran and Grandad, Rosemary and Billy Jewell. Thank you for imparting a love of cooking and eating. And for everything else.

CONTENTS

INTRODUCTION   6

A LITTLE BAKING PEP TALK   10
EQUIPMENT   12
MEASUREMENTS AND OVEN TEMPERATURE   14
INGREDIENTS   14
TECHNIQUES   18
WASTE   20
TIME   20
USE YOUR INTUITION   21
PIE BASICS   22

PASTRY   27

EARLY   55

MIDDAY   81

ALL DAY   111

LATER   147

PANTRY   187

INDEX   216
ABOUT THE AUTHORS   222
ACKNOWLEDGEMENTS   223

Why write a book about savoury baking? Well, I am a chef who learned to bake, and this offering is a natural expression of my combined professional experiences. There are many beautiful books on sweet bakes, but it's harder to find one that focuses entirely on savoury bakes.

Savoury baking is practical and useful for our everyday lives. It is a great way to highlight vegetables and celebrate the joy of eating seasonally, while referencing great baking traditions. We are craving comfort and sustenance in an increasingly uncertain world, and savoury baking provides both of those. This is a style of cooking that stretches our creativity at the same time as being deeply soothing. It has almost endless scope for variation and visual flair and is fitting for any occasion.

Being rooted in tradition, savoury baking provides a profound sense of connection with place. Some bakes help form the identity of the villages from which they came, like the famous Melton Mowbray pork pies. Being from Cornwall, savoury baking is ingrained in my history and culture. Every Friday, my Gran would make a pasty tart for the family to share, creating not only strong family connections as we sat around the table together, but treasured childhood memories, too. Each time I make it now, I am transported back in time.

When Pippa and I owned our bakery, Tivoli Road, many of our savoury bakes had an almost cult-like following. People queued not just for the bread, doughnuts and croissants, but for the savoury offerings: breakfast rolls, pies, sausage rolls and more. I love using my restaurant experience to inform seasoning and flavour combinations to create full-flavoured dishes. Our first book, *The Tivoli Road Baker*, included a small selection of our savoury repertoire, and one of the highlights of that book was the wonderful feedback from people who said how much they used those recipes and loved them.

In our twenty years together, the way we eat has changed a lot. Our first date was at Phil Howard's two-Michelin-starred restaurant, The Square; these days, we have a young child and eat mostly at home. We grow a little food, and we go to the farmers' market each week before planning what we'll cook. When we do eat out, we like to support local businesses that we know are buying direct from the little guys.

Respecting and appreciating seasonal changes challenges us to be more creative with our cooking and provides opportunity for a more mindful way of baking. We make the most of what we have to hand to make nourishing and interesting bakes to eat now, and preserve seasonal gluts so we can enjoy them later.

Eating this way, we get to support small businesses that are farming in a regenerative way and, importantly, we are opting out of the industrial food system. By choosing to eat local food we are directly supporting our community rather than some far off billionaire. We recognise our privilege in being able to spend our time and money this way, but we do all have choices about where our money is spent, and this power is cumulative.

Don't feel like you need to have it 'right' all the time – know that you can make a difference in challenging a food system that is making us, and our planet, sick.

We know that diversity is critical to our health; actively seek ways to diversify what you're baking. Get curious about different grains and use at least some of them whole. Aside from the nutritional benefits, the flavour that you get from fresh whole grains makes your food so much more interesting.

Like many people, we are increasingly alarmed about the climate crisis we're living in. This concern is guiding many of our decisions, including what and where we eat. We're eating less meat overall and much less meat from hooved, methane-producing animals. In Australia, more sustainable meat sources include wild native animals like kangaroo and wallaby, or pests such as rabbits. Load up on whatever veggies are abundant in their season. Be curious and never stop learning.

In the kitchen, once you've mastered one technique, you can adapt it to create new and unique dishes using what you have to hand. The beetroot tarte tatin is a weeknight favourite at our house, but we certainly don't always use beetroot. It's great with just shallots or any combination of root vegetables. It will work well with gluten-free or vegan pastry. As you gain confidence with baking techniques, you are limited only by your imagination. Slow down and observe the processes, and you may find that the confines of your pantry or market garden are actually liberating you from a tyranny of choice.

I have always loved a simpler style of cooking. Starting with great ingredients and not playing around with them too much highlights produce at its peak and lets the food do the talking. I find in baking that less is more, preferring to use one or two flavours to complement a base ingredient and then lifting them with herbs and subtle spices. Using a recipe as a guide, I love the challenge of finding a great substitute if I'm missing something. You never know when you'll strike gold!

As we write this book, we are locked down in the middle of the COVID-19 pandemic. It's been wonderful to see more people baking at home, using produce from their local market or vegetable boxes. Long may it continue. In the speed of modern life we are losing skills, outsourcing the making of food and losing connection to our place and time in the world. When we take the time to make puff pastry from scratch or to ferment limes for pickle, we become intrinsically linked to our food. This situation has also highlighted the need to support local farmers and help one another. When the restaurants closed, it was heartening to see them supporting their suppliers by creating produce boxes, becoming the conduit for getting their produce out to the public in a new way.

So, we present this book – a collection of recipes gathered over many years, drawing on experience working in restaurants, cafes and bakeries, and taking inspiration from what we enjoy eating at home. Here you'll find some recipes that are quick enough for a school night dinner and others that are more involved. The Pantry chapter contains staples to use in or alongside your bakes, and these are some of my favourite recipes. They allow you to preserve and extend your favourite season in your own kitchen, or to make gifts for friends. The gift of food is so caring and loving; it's like offering a piece of yourself to share with others.

We hope you enjoy this little gift, from our hearts and kitchen to yours.

CONTENTS

INTRODUCTION 6

A LITTLE BAKING PEP TALK   10
EQUIPMENT   12
MEASUREMENTS AND OVEN TEMPERATURE   14
INGREDIENTS   14
TECHNIQUES   18
WASTE   20
TIME   20
USE YOUR INTUITION   21
PIE BASICS   22

PASTRY 27

EARLY 55

MIDDAY 81

ALL DAY 111

LATER 147

PANTRY 187

INDEX   216
ABOUT THE AUTHORS   222
ACKNOWLEDGEMENTS   223

Why write a book about savoury baking? Well, I am a chef who learned to bake, and this offering is a natural expression of my combined professional experiences. There are many beautiful books on sweet bakes, but it's harder to find one that focuses entirely on savoury bakes.

Savoury baking is practical and useful for our everyday lives. It is a great way to highlight vegetables and celebrate the joy of eating seasonally, while referencing great baking traditions. We are craving comfort and sustenance in an increasingly uncertain world, and savoury baking provides both of those. This is a style of cooking that stretches our creativity at the same time as being deeply soothing. It has almost endless scope for variation and visual flair and is fitting for any occasion.

Being rooted in tradition, savoury baking provides a profound sense of connection with place. Some bakes help form the identity of the villages from which they came, like the famous Melton Mowbray pork pies. Being from Cornwall, savoury baking is ingrained in my history and culture. Every Friday, my Gran would make a pasty tart for the family to share, creating not only strong family connections as we sat around the table together, but treasured childhood memories, too. Each time I make it now, I am transported back in time.

When Pippa and I owned our bakery, Tivoli Road, many of our savoury bakes had an almost cult-like following. People queued not just for the bread, doughnuts and croissants, but for the savoury offerings: breakfast rolls, pies, sausage rolls and more. I love using my restaurant experience to inform seasoning and flavour combinations to create full-flavoured dishes. Our first book, *The Tivoli Road Baker*, included a small selection of our savoury repertoire, and one of the highlights of that book was the wonderful feedback from people who said how much they used those recipes and loved them.

In our twenty years together, the way we eat has changed a lot. Our first date was at Phil Howard's two-Michelin-starred restaurant, The Square; these days, we have a young child and eat mostly at home. We grow a little food, and we go to the farmers' market each week before planning what we'll cook. When we do eat out, we like to support local businesses that we know are buying direct from the little guys.

Respecting and appreciating seasonal changes challenges us to be more creative with our cooking and provides opportunity for a more mindful way of baking. We make the most of what we have to hand to make nourishing and interesting bakes to eat now, and preserve seasonal gluts so we can enjoy them later.

Eating this way, we get to support small businesses that are farming in a regenerative way and, importantly, we are opting out of the industrial food system. By choosing to eat local food we are directly supporting our community rather than some far off billionaire. We recognise our privilege in being able to spend our time and money this way, but we do all have choices about where our money is spent, and this power is cumulative.

A LITTLE BAKING PEP TALK

I find you can add, take away or substitute ingredients more easily with savoury baking than with sweet, where precision is rewarded. So the aim in offering these recipes is that they can be used as a guide – switch up the pastries, filling or topping and create something uniquely yours.

For example, if you don't have rabbit, use chicken; if you don't have lentils, use quinoa; choose the pastry *you* like for your pie top or base. The vegan and gluten-free flaky pastries both work well to make a pasty, galette or sausage roll recipe. Pies can be made in small dishes for individual meals or in a large pan for a family pie. The only thing I wouldn't compromise on is the quality and provenance of the ingredients.

Before you make a recipe, take the time to sit down and read it through, either the night before or just before you start. Check you have all the ingredients and any special equipment required. Just a few minutes of reading and checking can save you time and frustration, especially if it's your first time making that recipe or you feel that it might challenge you. For example, I will take the butter for laminating puff pastry out of the fridge in advance, so when I'm ready to roll out the block, it's already at room temperature. I act like a TV chef, weighing up all the ingredients and placing them in order in front of me. To this day, I will reread and double-check the recipe as I'm cooking to make sure I haven't left out a step or forgotten an ingredient. It's an old habit, but it has saved me from quite a few potential disasters. Being prepared will make it a less stressful and more enjoyable cooking experience overall.

You will make mistakes along the way, but that's OK, we all do. Embrace your mistakes and keep going, as that is the only way you are going to improve. More is learned from mistakes than success. Write down what went wrong and how you'd do it differently next time. Don't stop after one bad bake; keep improving and learning along the way.

EQUIPMENT

I find the best equipment for making pastry is my hands, a good rolling pin and my kitchen benchtop. A lot of pastry can be made with just these things, but if you're going to invest in baking equipment, there are some things to consider.

I love my traditional, or 'roller' style, **rolling pin**. It has handles at each end, attached to a central dowel, for the roller to rotate around. I find these better for pastry than the rod-style rolling pins, because they require less grunt and don't work the dough as much.

An **electric stand mixer** can speed up the job and make light work if you have one. But if you don't, you can still successfully make all of the pastries in this book by hand.

A **dough scraper** and a **pastry brush** are inexpensive but invaluable, always in use and by your side. A **measuring tape** or **ruler** will ensure you get the dimensions right when rolling out your pastry. Dimensions given are aimed at maximising the recipes and minimising pastry wastage.

A **portable digital timer** is essential. They are accurate, easy to use and if you leave the kitchen, you can take it with you.

I recommend using **digital scales** that measure to the gram. They are inexpensive and also save you having to wash up measuring spoons and cups countless times as you go.

In terms of the 'right' **pie dishes**, use what you already have. It might mean that you get more or fewer pies out of a recipe than me, but what you're really aiming for is flavour and texture.

The same goes for **pastry cutters**. At home I find myself using plates, mixing bowls or lids of various sizes as templates to cut out my pastry. Size doesn't matter!

All the recipes have been tested in a domestic electric **fan-forced oven** (see also page 14). However, ovens tend to have their own personalities, so times and temperatures may vary. Get to know your oven and use your baking intuition.

MEASUREMENTS AND OVEN TEMPERATURE

One of the best ways to guarantee a good bake is to ensure that you measure your ingredients correctly. Use reliable scales that measure to the gram, and be careful with your measuring cups and spoons. Standard measures for cups and spoons are frustratingly different in different countries. For example:

- in Australia, 1 tablespoon = 20 ml (¾ fl oz) and 1 cup = 250 ml (8½ fl oz);
- in the UK, 1 tablespoon = 15 ml (½ fl oz) and 1 cup = 284 ml (9½ fl oz);
- in the US, 1 tablespoon = 15 ml (½ fl oz) and 1 cup = 236 ml (8 fl oz).

I'm not sure why they can't all be the same! But this is why bakers prefer to measure ingredients by weight rather than volume. After all, 1 gram = 1 gram wherever you are in the world.

For some ingredients used in small amounts I have used volume measures; for example, herbs and spices. In my experience, savoury cooking requires less precision than bread, pastry or cake baking where pretty much everything is weighed. You need to be precise when making your pastry doughs, but fillings and toppings can be adjusted to taste.

All volume measures given in this book are based on Australian standard measures: 1 level tablespoon = 20 ml. Sometimes, measuring spoons purchased in Australia may be international measures, so it's worth checking that yours are 20 ml.

All recipes were tested in grams for accuracy. When converted to ounces, spoons and cups there may be variation. I recommend weighing ingredients in grams where possible.

All recipes in this book were tested in a domestic electric fan-forced oven. If using a conventional oven, increase the oven temperature by 20°C (70°F).

INGREDIENTS

FLOUR AND GRAIN

Plain (all-purpose) flour is used for most pastry doughs. It is low in protein, making dough that is softer and flakier. Flour can either be roller milled or stoneground. Roller-milled flour is more stable and has a long shelf life because it contains less of the germ, bran and oil from the grain. Stone milling retains more bran and germ, giving the flour more life and nutrition for you. It is less shelf-stable and best stored in the fridge, like any wholegrain flour.

Bakers (strong or bread) flour is mainly used for bread baking and is higher in protein, usually 10 per cent or more, though this varies from country to country. When bakers flour is mixed with water, strong gluten bonds are formed, making it easier to stretch and hold the gas produced by fermentation. This is what gives good bread a nice, open crumb.

You can use either plain or bakers flour to make pastry, but bear in mind the results will vary. For example, bakers flour will produce eye-catching results in puff pastry – think big flaky layers – but it will be chewier. Using plain flour will give you a softer mouthfeel, and you want this lightness in most cake or pastry baking. Some doughs, such as choux pastry, do benefit from using bakers flour to give you a good rise and holey centre. It's worthwhile understanding the differences so you can achieve the result you want.

I have included variations for using different wholegrain flours in the puff and flaky pastry doughs. Remember that wholegrain flours will absorb more liquid, and that different grains will perform slightly differently – this is not a bad thing! Add more liquid in small increments until your dough is the right consistency. Rye flour is not as binding as wheat, so it can be trickier to use, but with practice you can achieve a delicious rye puff pastry. I hope that once you experience the benefits of using whole grains, you will continue to experiment. Wholegrain flour even improves a simple béchamel, providing more flavour and nutrition.

I always use organic or biodynamic flour and grain from a reliable farm. This is important for soil heath and your health. I don't want to be eating grain farmed with chemical inputs; it is simply not good for our gut, immune system or overall health. There are many places now where you can buy good flour and grain in bulk, or ask your local baker for some.

EGGS

Always use truly free- (or open-) range eggs.

Varying egg sizes can really throw a recipe out, especially if you use a lot. All the recipes have been tested with medium eggs, about 50 g (1¾ oz) without the shell. I allow 20 g (¾ oz) for a yolk and 30 g (1 oz) for the white.

Egg wash is a mixture brushed onto pastry before baking to give the finished product a lovely golden shine and a little extra crispness and flakiness. It's used for many of the recipes in this book. I use:

1 whole egg
1 egg yolk
20 g (¾ oz/1 tablespoon) full-cream (whole) milk
a pinch of salt

Just whisk all the ingredients together. It will keep, refrigerated, in a sealed container for a few days. The salt helps to denature the proteins in the eggs so it's easier to brush the pastry.

Egg wash can also be used to fill holes or cracks in a pastry tart shell. Simply brush the surface of the shell in the last few minutes of blind baking to ensure any small holes are sealed. If the hole is too big, use a little piece of raw dough and use the egg wash like a cement to plug that hole, then blind bake for a further 5 minutes to seal.

BUTTER

I always use unsalted butter – preferably cultured – when making pastry, and add salt as needed to complete the dish. The only place for salted butter is spread on your bread. Cultured butter is made by fermenting the cream prior to churning – this introduces probiotics and increases complexity of flavour.

There are many good butter makers around the world, even in Australia now (this is quite a recent development). It's great if you can find a small maker local to you and get to know them and their product. Sometimes, cultured butter can have excess moisture or be a bit soft; this may be a flaw but can also reflect normal changes in the cream. As with all ingredients that have been given over to industrial-scale production, we've become used to absolute consistency at the expense of flavour and nutrition. Nature (and therefore natural produce) changes with the seasons. By tuning into these changes, you can use your intuition and adapt, becoming a better baker.

CREAM

I use pure cream for all the recipes in this book. It contains 35–45% fat and has no added stabilisers or gelatine.

SALT

There are many different types of salt around. I usually only have two in my kitchen – a fine pure salt and a flaky sea salt.

I use fine Australian Pink Lake salt in doughs and for seasoning quiche mixtures and braises. Here I am aiming to bring out the flavours, and I find that fine salt mixes through better than flaky salt. For doughs, it's important to use the weight of salt specified, as changing the amount of salt can affect the success of the outcome.

For finishing a dish just before serving, I add flaky sea salt because I love how the little orbs of salt 'lift' the dish as you're eating it. Seasoning is subjective, so remember to taste and taste again, and trust your own judgement.

Bear in mind that 1 teaspoon of fine salt will contain more salt than 1 teaspoon of flaky salt, so if in doubt use the gram weight rather than a volume measurement.

MEAT

Let's be honest: humans consume far too much meat, most of it industrially farmed. In this system, animals are treated like a product, fed with pellets and often treated with heart-breaking cruelty. The meat is pumped full of water – to trick us into thinking we're getting more for our money – and antibiotics that we then ingest. Livestock agriculture is one of the biggest contributors to our climate crisis on a global scale. The negative impacts of this system cannot be overstated.

I do not support or condone this type of production or consumption of meat or animal products.

Humans have evolved to eat meat, and some animals can bring immense environmental benefit to small-scale regenerative farms. Others are legitimate pests that upset the balance within an ecosystem. The issue of meat consumption is not simple, and given that we all must eat food, the reality is that our choices affect food systems in one way or another. We vote with our wallets. Therefore, I think it's imperative to educate yourself on the complexities of our food systems and make choices about what you eat that align with your values and support your health.

So, in our family we eat much less meat than we used to. We know the farmers or butchers we buy from and we trust their practices. Increasingly, we eat wild animals such as kangaroo or rabbit that are abundant. And we don't waste any of the animal, using every part before ensuring it is returned to the earth to feed the soils and create new life.

TECHNIQUES

ROLL WITH IT

The flaky pastry recipe used in this book makes enough dough to line two 23–25 cm (9–10 in) diameter, 3–4 cm (1¼–1½ in) deep tart shells. After lining your tin, keep the pastry trimmings to plug holes or cracks, using them with egg wash to ensure the base is well sealed (see page 15).

Before you first roll out your cooled and rested dough, bang it with a rolling pin, hard enough to leave some indentations. This makes it more pliable and easier to use (see page 33, image 9).

Before rolling out the dough, lightly dust your kitchen bench with flour. Use a light dusting of flour – too much and the pastry will move around a lot and the flour can get caked on; not enough and it can stick to the work surface, especially on a hot day. The best way to roll is away from you, applying an even pressure, but do not press downwards. While rolling, allow the rolling pin to move in a forward-rolling motion to ensure an even roll. Turn the pastry ninety degrees when you need to.

You may prefer to roll out your dough between two sheets of baking paper. It's then very easy to transfer the rolled-out pastry to your tin or dish.

BLIND BAKING QUICHE AND TART SHELLS

I use aluminium foil to blind bake my quiche shells, as it gets right into the corners. If you're careful, you can also reuse it. Baking paper is another alternative that works well and can be reused. I never use plastic wrap because chemicals from the plastic can leach into your food, especially when exposed to heat. I use granulated sugar for my pastry weights as it's cheap, heavy and gets into the corners nicely. Uncooked rice also works well.

Blind bake at 190°C (375°F) for 30 minutes and then remove the lining and weights. Reduce the oven to 160°C (320°F) and bake for a further 20 minutes, or until the whole shell is golden. If you find the middle puffs up, prick the pastry a few times with a fork. Check again for any cracks or holes and use leftover dough to seal any potential leaks.

SOURDOUGH STARTER

There are many wonderful books on sourdough baking, and I covered it in much more detail in my first book, *The Tivoli Road Baker*. If you've never used a sourdough culture, the Buckwheat English muffins (page 66) and the Olive, rosemary and sea salt focaccia (page 143) are both wonderful starting points. The recipe for the Rye sourdough crackers (page 127) is ideal for using up the inevitable excess of starter. You could ask a baking friend for a little of their healthy, active starter or try your luck at your local bakery. But it's not hard to make.

Note: If you want to accelerate the whole process, you can feed every 12 hours instead of every 24 hours.

Day 1

In a jar with a capacity of at least 330 ml (11½ fl oz), mix 20 g (¾ oz) of water at 26°C (79°F) with 15 g (½ oz) of wholegrain flour, then cover and leave in a warm place for 24 hours.

Day 2

When you open your jar there may be a bubble or two, but don't worry if there aren't any – they will come. You may also notice a slightly tangy smell. Add 20 g (¾ oz) of water at 26°C (79°F) and 15 g (½ oz) of wholegrain flour, then stir it in until thoroughly combined. Cover and leave in a warm place for 24 hours.

Day 3

When you open the jar you should see some tiny bubbles starting to appear. You may notice a slightly grassy or sweet tangy smell, as well as a more acidic smell, like vinegar. These are good signs and an indicator that you're on the right track. Add 20 g (¾ oz) of water at 26°C (79°F) and 15 g (½ oz) of wholegrain flour and stir to combine. Cover and leave in a warm place for 24 hours.

Day 4

By now you should have more tiny bubbles and the fermentation should be well and truly happening. You may notice stronger smells, such as bananas and wheat beer. Add 20 g (¾ oz) of water at 26°C (79°F) and 15 g (½ oz) of wholegrain flour and stir to combine. Cover and leave in a warm place for 24 hours.

Day 5

You should see lots of tiny bubbles on the surface of your starter and may notice quite a strong acidic scent, like vinegar, when you open the lid. The smell will be quite sweet and slightly tangy but will disappear when you feed the starter. Add 20 g (¾ oz) of water at 26°C (79°F) and 15 g (½ oz) of wholegrain flour and stir to combine. Your starter may even be ready by now or Day 6. Cover and leave in a warm place for 24 hours.

Day 6

The starter should be very bubbly and active by now, with a strong, slightly alcoholic smell of fermentation. It should be ready to use; if not, add 20 g (¾ oz) of water at 26°C (79°F) and 15 g (½ oz) of wholegrain flour and stir to combine. Cover and leave in a warm place for at least 12 hours.

Day 7 onwards

The starter is now ready to use and should have lots of tiny bubbles on the surface and throughout. If you're not using it immediately, you can discard all but 1 tablespoon for maintenance. Feed this with 20 g (¾ oz) of water at 26°C (79°F) and 15 g (½ oz) of flour and stir to combine.

WASTE

SCRAPS FOR SNACKS

I hate waste. You will likely find that you have a bit of pastry left over here and there if it's not all used up plugging holes. I always keep these scraps and use them to make snacks (or Sausages in scraps, page 136). If you want to build up your supply, just wrap it well and freeze until you're ready to use it.

Just push the scraps together and roll out the pastry. Cut into strips or squares and bake until it's golden, then use like a cracker as a base for whatever is in the fridge or pantry – cheese, pickles, hummus and more. Get creative and resourceful! One of the nicest quick snacks I've made was pumpkin purée with leftover roasted root vegetables on a strip of puff pastry. It made a quick and easy lunch while writing this book.

WRAPPING PASTRY

I don't use plastic wrap in the kitchen. Instead, I use beeswax wraps to wrap and rest pastry. If you're storing pastry, wrap it first in baking paper and then wrap it tightly with a beeswax wrap. They can be found at eco-type shops or at farmers' markets. There are also lots of tutorials online for making your own.

For freezing pastry, I use compostable plastic wrap and then put it in a sealed container that I label.

TIME

When you're making dough that requires folds, or laminating dough such as puff pastry, do rest it in the fridge between folds for at least 30 minutes, as instructed in the recipe. Don't skip this step; it helps the gluten in the dough to relax so it will be easier for you to roll out the pastry. It also chills the fats to increase your 'flake factor'.

Consider the cooking times given in the recipes as a guide. If you are assembling your bakes in smaller formats (for example, making mini sausage rolls for a party), this will alter your baking time, so set the timer for 10 minutes less and keep an eye on your bake. Similarly with sauces; if you make a half batch, the cooking time will be slightly reduced.

Get your oven ready before you preheat it – think about where your bake will sit in the oven and adjust the shelves accordingly. Allow at least 20 minutes for the oven to fully heat up. Preheating is essential, as the initial burst of heat evaporates moisture quickly, lifting the pastry to create beautiful flaky and golden layers. I find the top of my oven is the hottest, so I place my shelves high, and if baking on more than one tray I swap the bottom to the top (and vice versa) during the bake. Also, always rotate your trays from front to back during the bake to get a more consistent and even colour.

USE YOUR INTUITION

Your senses and your intuition are indispensable in the kitchen. Look, listen, smell, touch and taste frequently – create a connection to your food. No two bakes are the same: ingredients can vary seasonally, and changes in temperature and humidity can also alter outcomes. So being present in the kitchen makes a huge difference. Just like in life, but that's another book ...

When I teach people how to bake, I always emphasise the importance of sensory feedback, especially with doughs and sourdough baking. Start to ask yourself questions. Is that ready or does it need more time? Do I like it darker or lighter? Does it need more salt?

The more you can tune into your senses and question everything, the easier it becomes. Your confidence rises and your baking gets better. Embrace the process and the results will ultimately taste great.

PIE BASICS

ASSEMBLING AND BAKING YOUR PIES

Most of the pie recipes in this book can be made as either one family-sized pie or several individual pies. The notable exception is the pork pie, which is a traditional British staple from Melton Mowbray in Leicestershire. Pork pies are free-formed in hot water pastry and eaten cold. But more about that later ... We're here to talk about assembling delicious braises into hot pies for cold evenings or afternoons at the footy.

FAMILY OR POT PIES

For family-sized pies, I put the braise into a deep pie dish and top it with flaky shortcrust pastry (page 36). The pastry provides a textural contrast to the soft braise, and a delicious extra element to complete the dish. I find that puff pastry doesn't bake well over a large pie because of the time required to heat the dish through to the centre. It's too slow and doesn't puff well, giving an uneven and unsatisfying bake.

As a guide, use a half quantity of pastry to serve up to four people. Use a full quantity to serve up to eight. You can also use the lard pastry, vegan flaky or gluten-free flaky pastry (pages 38, 46, 48).

To assemble your family pie, roll the pastry 3 mm (⅛ in) thick and cut a large circle 3 cm (1¼ in) wider in diameter than your pie dish (or roll into your desired shape based on the dimensions of your pie dish). Avoid rolling the pastry too thin – you want the crust to have some body and plenty of flaky layers.

Place your cooled braise into the pie dish, then grease the rim with butter or oil. Lay the pastry over the top, then use your fingers to pinch or crimp around the edge, or use a fork to press it down.

Brush the entire surface with egg wash (page 15) and poke a hole in the middle to allow steam to release during baking. Put it in the fridge for 30 minutes to set the pastry while you preheat the oven for the bake.

INDIVIDUAL PIES

Individual pies require a little more work, and I like to use different pastries for the top and bottom. There are some advantages for baking smaller pies – they're great for picnics or outings and to have on hand in the freezer for those nights when you need an easy dinner option.

My preference for the pie base is savoury shortcrust pastry (page 40). A half quantity will make up to five pies and a full quantity will make six to ten. You can also use flaky shortcrust, vegan flaky or gluten-free flaky pastry (pages 36, 46, 48).

For the top, I like puff pastry (page 32). Again, a half quantity will make up to five pies and a full quantity will make six to ten. Flaky shortcrust, lard pastry, vegan flaky and gluten-free flaky pastry will also work well (see pages 36, 38, 46 and 48).

My individual pie dishes are little enamel bowls, 14 cm (5½ in) in diameter. You can use what you have or use disposable aluminium dishes.

Roll out the base pastry 3 mm (⅛ in) thick and cut out circles, 2 cm (¾ in) wider in diameter than the top of your individual pie dishes to help attach and seal the pastry lid (or roll into your desired shape based on the dimensions of your pie dish). If your pie dishes are very deep, allow more overlap to account for the depth. Cover the pastry and put it in the fridge until you're ready to assemble.

Roll out the top pastry 3–4 mm (⅛ in) thick and cut out shapes the same size as your pie dishes. Cover and refrigerate.

Once I have the pastry rolled and cut, I like to assemble a batch of pies in a production line – do each step to every pie before moving on to the next. First grease the tins with a little butter. Place a disc of the base pastry into each tin and press it well into the corners of the base, working around it with your fingertips or a piece of extra dough. Trim off any excess pastry from the edges.

Divide the cooled braise evenly between your dishes. Brush a little egg wash (page 15) around the exposed rim of the pastry, then place the pastry lid on top and use the heel of your hand to gently push out any excess air. Pinch the edges together with your thumb and forefinger to seal the pie.

Brush the tops with egg wash and poke a hole in the middle to allow steam to release during the bake. I like to add seeds, nuts or grains for extra flavour and texture. This also helps to identify which pie is which if you have a few different batches in the freezer and are a bit lax with labelling. Put the pies in the fridge for 30 minutes to set the pastry while you preheat the oven for the bake.

BAKING YOUR PIES

Preheat the oven to 190°C (375°F). For small pies, bake for 10 minutes, then reduce the oven to 180°C (360°F). Bake for a further 25–30 minutes, turning halfway through for an even bake. For large pies, bake for 10 minutes, then reduce the oven to 180°C (360°F). Bake for a further 35–40 minutes, turning halfway through for an even bake. If baking from frozen, add 10 minutes to these times. The pies are ready when the pastry is flaky and golden. Always rest your pies for 10 minutes before eating.

USE YOUR INTUITION

Your senses and your intuition are indispensable in the kitchen. Look, listen, smell, touch and taste frequently – create a connection to your food. No two bakes are the same: ingredients can vary seasonally, and changes in temperature and humidity can also alter outcomes. So being present in the kitchen makes a huge difference. Just like in life, but that's another book ...

When I teach people how to bake, I always emphasise the importance of sensory feedback, especially with doughs and sourdough baking. Start to ask yourself questions. Is that ready or does it need more time? Do I like it darker or lighter? Does it need more salt?

The more you can tune into your senses and question everything, the easier it becomes. Your confidence rises and your baking gets better. Embrace the process and the results will ultimately taste great.

PIE BASICS

ASSEMBLING AND BAKING YOUR PIES

Most of the pie recipes in this book can be made as either one family-sized pie or several individual pies. The notable exception is the pork pie, which is a traditional British staple from Melton Mowbray in Leicestershire. Pork pies are free-formed in hot water pastry and eaten cold. But more about that later ... We're here to talk about assembling delicious braises into hot pies for cold evenings or afternoons at the footy.

FAMILY OR POT PIES

For family-sized pies, I put the braise into a deep pie dish and top it with flaky shortcrust pastry (page 36). The pastry provides a textural contrast to the soft braise, and a delicious extra element to complete the dish. I find that puff pastry doesn't bake well over a large pie because of the time required to heat the dish through to the centre. It's too slow and doesn't puff well, giving an uneven and unsatisfying bake.

As a guide, use a half quantity of pastry to serve up to four people. Use a full quantity to serve up to eight. You can also use the lard pastry, vegan flaky or gluten-free flaky pastry (pages 38, 46, 48).

To assemble your family pie, roll the pastry 3 mm (⅛ in) thick and cut a large circle 3 cm (1¼ in) wider in diameter than your pie dish (or roll into your desired shape based on the dimensions of your pie dish). Avoid rolling the pastry too thin – you want the crust to have some body and plenty of flaky layers.

Place your cooled braise into the pie dish, then grease the rim with butter or oil. Lay the pastry over the top, then use your fingers to pinch or crimp around the edge, or use a fork to press it down.

Brush the entire surface with egg wash (page 15) and poke a hole in the middle to allow steam to release during baking. Put it in the fridge for 30 minutes to set the pastry while you preheat the oven for the bake.

INDIVIDUAL PIES

Individual pies require a little more work, and I like to use different pastries for the top and bottom. There are some advantages for baking smaller pies – they're great for picnics or outings and to have on hand in the freezer for those nights when you need an easy dinner option.

My preference for the pie base is savoury shortcrust pastry (page 40). A half quantity will make up to five pies and a full quantity will make six to ten. You can also use flaky shortcrust, vegan flaky or gluten-free flaky pastry (pages 36, 46, 48).

For the top, I like puff pastry (page 32). Again, a half quantity will make up to five pies and a full quantity will make six to ten. Flaky shortcrust, lard pastry, vegan flaky and gluten-free flaky pastry will also work well (see pages 36, 38, 46 and 48).

g UN-
ALTED
UTTER

PASTRY

9 ESSENTIAL PASTRY STAPLES
PAGES 28-53

10g SA

PASTRY

Here is your basics toolkit, so that you can pick a pastry to suit your project and preferences. There are gluten-free and vegan pastry recipes that work well across a number of bakes, as well as my trusty and versatile flaky shortcrust. I use this as a light flaky base for free-form galettes or blind baked for quiche. Also included are my tried-and-true puff pastry, hot water pastry for free-form pies, light-as-air choux and delicious, rich brioche. The lard pasty pastry is an old family recipe. My Gran made it with lard and margarine, but I use lard and butter; you could also just use butter.

I love using a variety of fresh wholegrain flours for increased nutrition and for their distinctive flavours. Different flours perform differently, so I have included variations to guide you. I also like to vary the liquids I use, be it buttermilk, sour cream or milk kefir. Once you build a little confidence with the recipes, you can check and adjust the hydration as you go.

When I make pastry at home, I tend to make it in batches and freeze the excess for a quick bake next time around. My number one tip for great flaky pastry is to make it by hand and use a rolling pin to break the butter into the flour until just combined, and then rest it. This reduces the risk of overworking your dough.

I appreciate that not everyone has the time or inclination to make everything from scratch, so if you choose to buy pastry rather than make it, I offer two pieces of advice: reference this chapter to find out the weight in grams of pastry required for your bake so you know what you need to buy, and buy real pastry made from real ingredients. Many pastries in the supermarket are made with margarine instead of butter and include stabilisers and emulsifiers. In Australia, I recommend Carême pastry – they use free-range eggs and natural ingredients and even make a wholemeal spelt puff. If you have a great local bakery, you could ask them if they sell pastry for home use.

PUFF PASTRY
MAKES 830 G (1 LB 13 OZ)

Puff pastry can look spectacular and has many uses. Making it is not as difficult as you might think. In particular, the perception that it's time-consuming can be off-putting; it does take time, but it's short bursts of work punctuated by long rests. I recommend breaking down the process into small chunks: prepare the dough and butter block two days before you want to bake, laminate the butter into the dough the next day, then let it rest overnight in the fridge before using.

This recipe is tried and tested and gives excellent results. It is set up so that you can use a standard 250 g (9 oz) block of butter. It may make more pastry than you need, but if you are going to invest the time to make it, you'll be thankful that you've got some ready to go for next time and, once made, it freezes really well.

Take note of the weather and observe how the butter is performing. If it's too soft, it might need more time in the fridge between folds; if it's too hard, it will crack. The vinegar helps to prevent discolouration and also helps with the gluten cross-linking.

DAY 1
Take the 70 g (2½ oz) butter out of the fridge, cut it into 1 cm (½ in) cubes and leave to soften slightly for 10 minutes before you start – you want it to be cold but pliable.

Combine the water and vinegar in a jug. Put the flour, salt and butter cubes in the bowl of a stand mixer fitted with the paddle attachment. Mix on low speed to break the butter into the flour until you have shards of butter the size of rolled oats still visible. With the mixer running, slowly pour in the vinegar mixture and mix until the dough just comes together. You don't want any dry pieces, but you need to be careful not to overwork the dough.

Flatten the dough into a rectangle about 1 cm (½ in) thick. Wrap the dough and rest it in the fridge for 2 hours, or overnight.

Meanwhile, prepare the butter for laminating. Place the butter block between two sheets of baking paper and use a rolling pin to roll it into a rectangle roughly measuring 18 × 20 cm (7 × 8 in). Put the butter in the fridge, between the sheets of baking paper, and refrigerate for 2 hours, or overnight.

70 g (2½ oz) unsalted butter, chilled
150 g (5½ oz) chilled water
10 g (⅓ oz/2 teaspoons) white vinegar
340 g (12 oz) plain (all-purpose) flour
10 g (⅓ oz) fine salt

FOR LAMINATING
250 g (9 oz) block unsalted butter, at room temperature

WHOLEMEAL VARIATION
70 g (2½ oz) unsalted butter, chilled
180 g (6½ oz) chilled water
10 g (⅓ oz/2 teaspoons) white vinegar
170 g (6 oz) wholemeal (whole-wheat) flour
170 g (6 oz) plain (all-purpose) flour
10 g (⅓ oz) fine salt

RECIPE CONTINUES

DAY 2

Remove the dough and rolled-out butter from the fridge about 30 minutes before you laminate the pastry. You want the butter to be malleable but not too soft.

Lightly dust your kitchen bench with flour. Lay the dough rectangle on the bench with one short side parallel with the edge of the bench. Roll the dough away from you to form a rectangle measuring 20 × 40 cm (8 × 15¾ in), still with the short side closest to you.

Place the butter block in the middle of the dough, with the 20 cm (8 in) side of the butter parallel with the bench. Fold both free short sides of the dough over the top of the butter so they meet in the middle, encasing the butter. Lightly pinch the ends together to seal (the seam should run parallel with the bench).

Rotate the dough block 90 degrees so the seam is now perpendicular to the bench. Using your rolling pin, gently press or stamp along the length of the dough to make it more malleable (you can do this at any stage in the process to make the dough easier to work with). Next, roll the dough away from you to form a 20 × 40 cm (8 × 15¾ in) rectangle, again with one short side parallel with the bench. Starting from the side closest to you, fold the bottom third of the dough into the middle, then the top third over the top of that, as if folding a letter. Refrigerate for 20 minutes.

Put your dough on the bench with the open seam on your right-hand side and perpendicular to the edge of the bench. Roll the dough away from you to form a 20 × 40 cm (8 × 15¾ in) rectangle. Fold the bottom third of the dough into the middle, then the top third over the top of that, as if folding a letter. Repeat this step until you have completed four single (or letter) folds in total. Refrigerate your pastry for 1 hour after every two folds to keep the butter from getting too soft (refrigerate for 30 minutes after every fold if it's a warm day). If you have kept the pastry in the fridge for more than 1 hour, allow to stand for 10–15 minutes before continuing (reduce this time in hot weather).

Once all four folds are done, wrap your pastry and rest it in the fridge for at least 6 hours, or preferably overnight, before you use it. Chilling the pastry before using it prevents it from shrinking. Roll it out to whatever thickness you need. The pastry will keep for 3–4 days in the fridge, or up to 1 month in the freezer.

The pictured pies were made using plain puff pastry for the tops.

WHOLE RYE VARIATION

70 g (2½ oz) unsalted butter, chilled

180 g (6½ oz) chilled water

10 g (⅓ oz/2 teaspoons) white vinegar

135 g (5 oz) rye flour or wholegrain rye flour

205 g (7 oz) plain (all-purpose) flour

10 g (⅓ oz) fine salt

FLAKY SHORTCRUST PASTRY

MAKES 700 G (1 LB 9 OZ)

This has been my go-to pastry for years. It's perfect for lots of my favourite bakes, such as galettes, quiche or tops for pot pies. It is very easy to make and use, and it gives you a wonderfully light, flaky crust.

To increase the versatility, I have included variations for wholemeal and whole rye. Try any grains you can get your hands on and celebrate the difference in flavours.

If you want to add even more flavour, substitute the water with crème fraîche, sour cream or milk kefir. When using wholemeal or rye, the absorbency of the flour will differ, so check the dough as you mix and add more liquid if needed.

I recommend making the plain dough first so you get to know how the dough should feel. Once you're comfortable with that, you can change the flours and liquids used, knowing what you're aiming for.

Cut the butter into 1 cm (½ in) cubes and chill it in the freezer while you weigh up the rest of your ingredients.

Put the flour and salt in a mound on your kitchen bench and scatter the chilled butter cubes over the top. Use a rolling pin to roll the butter into the flour, gathering the flour back into the middle as you go with a dough scraper or spatula. Keep rolling until the mixture is crumbly with shards of butter the size of rolled oats still visible.

Make a well in the middle and add the chilled water. Use a dough scraper or knife to gently cut the flour into the water, gathering up any leaks as you do, until you have an even crumbly texture. Use your fingertips to gently push it all together into a rough dough with a slightly sticky texture. If it feels dry, add more water, 1 tablespoon at a time, until there are no floury bits left.

Roll out or press the dough into a rectangle 2–3 cm (¾ –1¼ in) thick (exact dimensions are not important here). Fold one-third of the dough into the middle, then the other third over the top of that, as if folding a letter. Rotate the dough 90 degrees and roll it out again into a rectangle 2–3 cm (¾ –1¼ in) thick, then repeat the letter fold. Don't worry about making these folds perfectly neat – this is just to finish bringing the dough together and layering the butter, which results in a lovely flakiness.

Rotate and roll out the dough once more into a rectangle 2–3 cm (¾ –1¼ in) thick and do one last fold. Wrap and refrigerate for at least 1 hour, or overnight. The pastry will keep for 4–5 days in the fridge, or up to 3 months in the freezer.

The pictured dough was made using whole spelt flour.

225 g (8 oz) unsalted butter, chilled
350 g (12½ oz) plain (all-purpose) flour
6 g (⅕ oz/1 teaspoon) fine salt
120 g (4½ oz) chilled water

WHOLEMEAL VARIATION
225 g (8 oz) unsalted butter, chilled
250 g (9 oz) wholemeal (whole-wheat) or spelt flour
100 g (4 oz) plain (all-purpose) flour
6 g (⅕ oz/1 teaspoon) fine salt
140 g (5 oz) chilled water

WHOLE RYE VARIATION
225 g (8 oz) unsalted butter, chilled
180 g (6½ oz) rye flour or wholegrain rye flour
170 g (6 oz) plain (all-purpose) flour
6 g (⅕ oz/1 teaspoon) fine salt
140 g (5 oz) chilled water

Wholegrain flours absorb more liquid than plain. If you find the dough too dry, add extra water, 1 tablespoon at a time, until you have the correct consistency.

LARD SHORTCRUST PASTRY

MAKES 1.3 KG (2 LB 14 OZ)

This is a traditional Cornish pasty pastry. My Gran used to make this lard pastry every week for our pasties or pasty tarts, so it's an incredibly well-used and proven recipe. It's also wonderfully easy to work with; if it tears, you can simply stretch a little excess over the rip and carry on. The lard and butter provide lots of flavour, making it a good option for almost any savoury bake.

I have added a wholemeal variation because I love the flavour of whole grains. Another traditional variation is to use beef dripping instead of lard, resulting in a different flavour and crisper finish. You can of course also just use all butter in the recipe.

———

Put the flour and salt in a mound on your kitchen bench and scatter the chilled butter and lard cubes over the top. Use a rolling pin to roll the fats into the flour, gathering the flour back into the middle as you go with a dough scraper or spatula. Keep rolling until the mixture has a crumbly texture, with shards of butter the size of rolled oats still visible.

Make a well in the middle and add the chilled water. Continue using the dough scraper to fold the flour over the water and gently work it in with your hands, working from the outside in, until the dough just comes together. The dough should be firm and not sticky to the touch.

Roll out or press the dough into a rectangle 2–3 cm (¾ –1¼ in) thick (exact dimensions are not important here). Fold one-third of the dough into the middle, then the other third over the top of that, as if folding a letter. Rotate the dough 90 degrees and roll it out again into a rectangle 2–3 cm (¾ –1¼ in) thick, then repeat the letter fold. Don't worry about making these folds perfectly neat – this is just to finish bringing the dough together and layering the butter, which results in a lovely flakiness.

Fold the dough over itself a few times to create rough layers. Shape it into a flat block, then wrap and put it in the fridge to rest for at least 2 hours, or preferably overnight, before using. The pastry will keep for 3–4 days in the fridge, or up to 3 months in the freezer.

700 g (1 lb 9 oz) plain (all-purpose) flour
6 g (⅕ oz/1 teaspoon) fine salt
175 g (6 oz) unsalted butter, chilled and cut into 1 cm (½ in) cubes
175 g (6 oz) lard, chilled and cut into 1 cm (½ in) cubes
270 g (9½ oz) chilled water

WHOLEMEAL VARIATION

350 g (12½ oz) wholemeal (whole-wheat) flour
350 g (12½ oz) plain (all-purpose) flour
6 g (⅕ oz/1 teaspoon) fine salt
175 g (6 oz) unsalted butter, chilled and cut into 1 cm (½ in) cubes
175 g (6 oz) lard, chilled and cut into 1 cm (½ in) cubes
280 g (10 oz) chilled water

Wholemeal (whole-wheat) flour will absorb more liquid than plain. If you find the dough too dry, you can add extra water, 1 tablespoon at a time as you are completing your dough, until you have the correct consistency.

SAVOURY SHORTCRUST PASTRY
MAKES 560 G (1 LB 4 OZ)

This is the pastry I use for all savoury pie bases, whether for individual pies or a large one. Being very sturdy, it can also be used as a base for quiches. The leftover dough or trimmings can be used again until they are used up, although the texture will change. It's very easy to make, and is therefore a good pastry introduction for children learning alongside you.

Once made, the dough will set hard because it has lots of butter, so take it out of the fridge at least an hour before you roll it so that it's malleable without being soft.

Combine the water and vinegar in a jug. Put the flour and salt in a mound on your kitchen bench and scatter the chilled butter over the top. Use a rolling pin to roll the butter into the flour, gathering the flour back into the middle as you go with a dough scraper or spatula.

Make a well in the middle and add the water and vinegar mixture. Continue using the dough scraper to fold the flour over the liquid and gently work it in with your hands, working from the outside in, until the dough just comes together. The dough should be firm and not sticky to the touch.

Roll out or press the dough into a rectangle 2–3 cm (¾ –1¼ in) thick (exact dimensions are not important here). Fold one-third of the dough into the middle, then the other third over the top of that, as if folding a letter. Rotate the dough 90 degrees and roll it out again into a rectangle 2–3 cm (¾ –1¼ in) thick, then repeat the letter fold. Don't worry about making these folds perfectly neat – this is just to finish bringing the dough together and layering the butter, which results in a lovely flakiness.

Flatten the dough into a rectangle about 2 cm (¾ in) thick. Wrap the dough and rest it in the fridge for at least 1 hour, or overnight, before using. The pastry will keep for 1 week in the fridge, or up to 3 months in the freezer.

If you prefer to use a stand mixer to make this dough, put the flour, salt and butter cubes in the bowl of the mixer fitted with the paddle attachment. Mix on low speed to break the butter into the flour until you have shards of butter still visible and the mixture starts to look yellow.

With the mixer running, slowly pour in the vinegar mixture and mix until the dough just comes together. You don't want any dry pieces, but you need to be careful not to overwork it. You can add a bit more water if you have any dry clumps, but don't let the dough get sticky.

Proceed with the above rolling and shaping instructions from here.

110 g (4 oz) water, at room temperature
10 g (⅓ oz/2 teaspoons) white vinegar
320 g (11½ oz) plain (all-purpose) flour
10 g (⅓ oz) fine salt
110 g (4 oz) unsalted butter, chilled and cut into 1 cm (½ in) cubes

HOT WATER PASTRY
MAKES 1.3 KG (2 LB 14 OZ)

Hot water pastry is traditionally used for pork pies. The dough is mixed while the water and fats are hot, and then chilled. You end up with a pastry that is sturdy and easy to work with – great for hand-forming any kind of raised pie.

For a vegetarian version, use all butter instead of lard. This pastry it best used the day it's made.

———

Put the butter, lard and water in a medium saucepan over a medium heat and stir until melted. Bring to a simmer, then remove the pan from the heat.

Put the flour, salt and eggs in the bowl of a stand mixer fitted with the paddle attachment. Mix on medium speed until thoroughly combined. With the mixer running on medium speed, pour the hot butter mixture into the flour mixture in a steady stream. Mix for 3–4 minutes until the dough comes together, then tip it out onto a lightly floured kitchen bench and knead for 1–2 minutes. Form the dough into a ball and place it in a bowl. Cover with a damp tea towel (dish towel). Rest at room temperature for 1 hour.

Tip the dough onto the bench and knead for 1 minute, then return it to the bowl and cover. Put in the fridge to rest for up to 1 hour before using. If chilled for longer than this, you may find that the pastry is too firm to use; in this case, leave it at room temperature for 20 minutes to make it more pliable.

130 g (4½ oz) unsalted butter, cut into 2 cm (¾ in) cubes
130 g (4½ oz) lard, cut into 2 cm (¾ in) cubes
250 g (9 oz) water
675 g (1½ lb) plain (all-purpose) flour
10 g (⅓ oz) fine salt
100 g (3½ oz/2 medium) eggs

CHOUX PASTRY

MAKES 400 G (14 OZ)

Making choux pastry is not difficult but it does require precision in timing, adding the flour just as the butter comes to the boil, then cooking out the flour just enough. But then you can allow the oven to do the rest, ensuring that steam is trapped in to the end of the bake. The steam creates the leavening, and the heat from the oven will also set the flour and egg proteins once it has risen, which gives you the holey centre. So don't be tempted to open the oven door too soon.

This is a classic choux pastry used to make chocolate éclairs, profiteroles and savoury Gougères (page 141).

Combine the water, butter and salt in a heavy-based medium saucepan over a medium heat. Melt the butter, stirring occasionally to incorporate all the ingredients.

Bring the mixture to the boil, then, just as it boils, add the flour all at once. Mix well with a wooden spoon as you cook out the starch in the flour and form your dough. Reduce the heat to low and continue to cook the dough, stirring constantly, for about 2 minutes, or until it comes away from the side of the pan. The starch in the flour hydrates and binds with the liquid, which stabilises the mixture. It is important that you don't overcook the dough at this stage, otherwise the proteins in the flour denature and the flour will not hold the liquid or eggs.

Transfer the dough to a stand mixer fitted with the paddle attachment. Beat on medium speed for 1 minute, then add the eggs, a little at a time, ensuring that each addition is well incorporated before adding the next. This should take about 2 minutes and result in a smooth, shiny dough. (This step can also be done by hand, adding the eggs into the saucepan, a little at a time, and beating well with a wooden spoon.) The choux pastry is ready to use straight away. It will keep, covered, in the fridge for 2–3 days.

150 g (5½ oz) water
70 g (2½ oz) unsalted butter, chopped
3 g (⅒ oz/½ teaspoon) fine salt
80 g (2¾ oz) bakers (strong) flour, sifted
100 g (3½ oz/2 medium) eggs, lightly beaten

VEGAN FLAKY PASTRY
MAKES 800 G (1 LB 12 OZ)

I'm a firm believer in baking being accessible to everyone, and that most things can be tweaked to meet any dietary requirements. This pastry will provide a great base for galettes, quiche, pies and even sausage rolls.

In conventional flaky pastry, butter provides lovely layers and flakiness in the finished bake. You want to leave little lumps of butter in the dough to provide moisture during baking, to create rise and delicate flakiness. Here, I've used a homemade vegan butter and applied the same principle. The result is a delicious pastry, and even without butter it's still flaky and eminently versatile.

Make the vegan butter a day before you make the pastry to give it time to set in the fridge. The nutritional yeast provides a colour similar to butter and a gentle umami flavour, but the pastry will work fine without it.

___

DAY 1
To make the vegan butter, heat the coconut oil in a small saucepan over a low heat until just melted. Take the pan off the heat and whisk in the olive oil, milk, vinegar and nutritional yeast, if using. Set aside, occasionally whisking the mixture until it cools and forms a thick paste. Refrigerate in a sealed container overnight.

DAY 2
To make the pastry, put the flour, salt and butter cubes in the bowl of a stand mixer fitted with the paddle attachment. Mix on medium speed until well combined but with shards of butter the size of rolled oats still visible.

With the mixer running, add the liquid and mix for 30–60 seconds until the dough just comes together. The dough should not be sticky and you should still see pieces of butter.

Tip the dough onto a lightly floured kitchen bench and fold it a few times to help build up layers. To do this, take half of the dough and pull it up and over itself, then push down on it. Repeat this a few times and then shape the dough into a slab. Wrap and refrigerate for at least 1 hour, or overnight.

Roll the pastry between two sheets of baking paper to the required shape and thickness, then wrap and return it to the fridge for 1 hour before using. Allowing the butter to set into the pastry will give you a flakier result. The pastry will keep for 1 week in the fridge, or up to 3 months in the freezer.

Before baking, instead of using egg wash, brush the pastry with a little water or plant-based milk to help with colour, rise and flakiness.

VEGAN BUTTER
160 g (5½ oz) refined deodorised coconut oil
30 g (1 oz) light olive oil
50 g (1¾ oz) soy or plant-based milk
4 g (⅛ oz) apple-cider vinegar
2 g (⅟₁₆ oz/1½ teaspoons) nutritional yeast (optional)

PASTRY
400 g (14 oz) plain (all-purpose) flour
8 g (¼ oz) fine salt
240 g (8½ oz) vegan butter (see above), chilled and cut into 1 cm (½ in) cubes
150 g (5½ oz) chilled plant-based milk or water

GLUTEN-FREE FLAKY PASTRY

MAKES 1 KG (2 LB 3 OZ)

I had never made gluten-free pastry before researching for this book, and won't deny I was wondering how on earth I was going to do it well. After a lot of research and trial and error, I finally have a recipe that tastes good and performs well. It can be used to make galettes or pies and is excellent for sausage rolls.

The technique used here is similar to making puff pastry by laminating a butter sheet into the dough. I do four folds to build up layers of butter through the dough. If your dough feels a bit tough when you first start laminating it, use your rolling pin to beat the dough a little to make it more pliable.

One benefit of not having gluten in the dough is that you don't need to rest it between folds to allow the protein bonds to relax. So once you've made the dough and prepared your butter sheet, you can chill them and then do all the folds at once. However, there is a caveat: in a warm kitchen you might find that the butter starts to melt; in this case, cover and refrigerate the dough after a couple of folds to firm up the butter a little.

———

Combine the tapioca starch, potato starch, pea flour, brown rice flour, sorghum flour, xanthan gum and salt in the bowl of a stand mixer fitted with the dough hook. Scatter over the butter cubes. Mix on medium speed until the mixture looks like breadcrumbs. With the mixer running, add the water and mix to bring it all together into a firm dough with the texture of playdough. It should have a slight stickiness; if it feels too dry, add more water, 1 tablespoon at a time, incorporating it fully between additions.

Tip the dough onto a lightly floured kitchen bench and knead it for 3–4 minutes, then shape it into a rectangle roughly measuring 18 × 20 cm (7 × 8 in). Cover and refrigerate the dough for 2 hours, or overnight.

Meanwhile, prepare the butter for laminating. Place the butter block between two sheets of baking paper and use a rolling pin to roll it into a rectangle roughly measuring 18 × 20 cm (7 × 8 in). Put the butter in the fridge, between the sheets of baking paper, and refrigerate for 2 hours, or overnight.

Remove the dough and rolled-out butter from the fridge 15 minutes before you laminate the pastry. You want the butter to be malleable but not too soft.

90 g (3 oz) tapioca starch
90 g (3 oz) potato starch
20 g (¾ oz) pea or soy flour
140 g (5 oz) brown rice flour, plus extra for dusting
70 g (2½ oz) sorghum flour
10 g (⅓ oz) xanthan gum
7 g (¼ oz) fine salt
100 g (3½ oz) unsalted butter, chilled and cut into 1 cm (½ in) cubes
230 g (8 oz) chilled water
250 g (9 oz) block unsalted butter, at room temperature, for laminating

RECIPE CONTINUES

Lightly dust your kitchen bench with rice flour. Lay the dough rectangle on the bench with one short side parallel with the edge of the bench. Roll the dough away from you to form a rectangle measuring 20 × 40 cm (8 × 15¾ in), still with the short side closest to you.

Place the butter block in the middle of the dough, with the 20 cm (8 in) side of the butter parallel with the bench. Fold both free short sides of the dough over the top of the butter so they meet in the middle, encasing the butter. Lightly pinch the ends together to seal (the seam should run parallel with the bench).

Rotate the dough block 90 degrees so the seam is now perpendicular to the bench. Using your rolling pin, gently press or stamp along the length of the dough to make it more malleable (you can do this at any stage in the process to make the dough easier to work with, see page 33, image 9 as well). Roll the dough away from you to form a 20 × 40 cm (8 × 15¾ in) rectangle, again with one short side parallel with the bench. Starting from the side closest to you, fold the bottom third of the dough into the middle, then the top third over the top of that, as if folding a letter. Rotate the dough 90 degrees anticlockwise, placing the open seam to the right. Repeat this step three more times, rotating the dough 90 degrees between each fold.

As mentioned, there's no need to rest the dough between folds; there is no gluten in the flour, so the dough will not shrink. However, you do need to be careful that the butter doesn't get too soft, especially in a warm kitchen. If it starts to feel too soft, put it in the fridge for 30 minutes after the second fold before proceeding.

Once all four folds are done, wrap your pastry and chill for at least 1 hour before use. Leave the pastry at room temperature for 15 minutes before you use it, to soften slightly. Roll the pastry between two sheets of baking paper to the required shape and thickness, then wrap and return it to the fridge for 1 hour before using. The pastry will keep for 5 days in the fridge, or up to 3 months in the freezer.

BRIOCHE
MAKES 660 G (1 LB 7 OZ)

I first made this buttery brioche when I was working in London at Pied à Terre, and it's been my go-to recipe since.

You can bake it in a tin to make slices of soft toasted brioche to serve with pâté, or form it into burger buns of any size. One recipe, many possibilities.

The most important thing to remember, apart from choosing great ingredients, is to maintain the dough temperature at around 22–24°C (72–75°F) from mixing to proving. If it gets too cool, you risk the butter 'setting' and weighing the dough down, resulting in a heavier, bread-like texture when baked. Brioche should have a soft, light, buttery texture.

This recipe can be made in one day, or you can make the dough and leave it to slow prove in the fridge overnight. Once baked, the brioche keeps well for a few days in an airtight container. It also freezes well – you can either toast it from frozen or refresh it in the oven for 6 minutes at 160°C (320°F).

---

320 g (11½ oz) bakers (strong) flour
40 g (1½ oz) soft brown sugar
5 g (⅛ oz) fine salt
150 g (5½ oz/3 medium) eggs, at room temperature
60 g (2 oz) full-cream (whole) milk
7 g (¼ oz/2 teaspoons) instant dried yeast or 15 g (½ oz) fresh yeast
80 g (2¾ oz) unsalted butter, at room temperature, cut into 1 cm (½ in) dice

Put the flour, sugar, salt, eggs, milk and yeast in the bowl of a stand mixer fitted with the dough hook. Mix on low speed for 5 minutes to incorporate the ingredients, stopping occasionally to scrape down the side of the bowl. Check the consistency – it should be like slightly sticky playdough.

Increase the speed to medium and mix for a further 5 minutes, then add the butter all at once. Don't worry about overcrowding the bowl – it will all work itself out and mix through.

Continue to mix on medium speed for 8 minutes. You may need to stop to scrape down the side of the bowl a few times. Mix until the dough comes away from the side of the bowl and is velvety and smooth; you should be able to stretch it out without breaking.

Cover and set aside for 1 hour, ideally at around 22–24°C (72–75°F) to allow the dough to rise. If the room is too cold, put the dough in your (cold) oven with the light on, with a small tray of hot water at the bottom to create warmth and humidity.

RECIPE CONTINUES

Now give the dough a fold. To do this, wet or oil your hands and grab a piece of dough on the side of the bowl. Pull and stretch it up and over the middle to the other side of the bowl. Repeat this six to eight times, moving around the edge of the bowl. (At this stage, you can cover and refrigerate the dough overnight if desired.)

Cover once more and set aside at room temperature to prove for another hour, or until the dough has risen and feels light and full of air – it should wobble a little if you gently shake the bowl.

To finish your brioche into rolls, see Bacon and egg breakfast buns (page 61). To prepare a brioche loaf, see Asparagus, ham and cheese bostocks (page 116).

GROUND BL
EPPER

EARLY

9 DELICIOUS WAYS TO START YOUR DAY
PAGES 56-79

EARLY

The morning is my favourite time of the day. I love being up before everyone else, in that early light when the day is full of promise and I can have a quiet moment to myself.

The recipes in this chapter are designed to keep your mornings hassle-free, whether you're after a quick bite before work or a slow Sunday brunch. Make the buckwheat English muffins the evening before and then wake up to fresh muffins that need just a little warmth and a slathering of butter. If you're organised, the scones or quiche can be made on a school morning, or even the night before. They make excellent lunch box fillers.

Even the more involved recipes can be made up ahead of time or are comprised of elements that can be prepared in advance. I love waking up on a Sunday knowing I have pastry rolled out for a breakfast galette of pear and black pudding – it takes just a few minutes to assemble. The ham and cheese palmiers are another favourite, pulled from the freezer and baked while I enjoy my coffee.

It's so easy to fall into a rut, and a simple shift can help break the routine and set up possibilities for each new day. I hope you find some inspiration here to bring variety and nourishment to your breakfast choices.

BACON AND EGG BREAKFAST BUNS
MAKES 12

There's nothing better than a bacon and egg bun first thing – even better when it's a brioche bun. Because mornings tend to be busy, I recommend you make the brioche dough ahead of time so it's ready to go.

These buns, along with a cup of coffee, were part of my morning ritual when we had Tivoli Road Bakery: a soft brioche bun, crispy bacon and a runny egg. It was so satisfying – and even better with tomato kasundi!

——

1 quantity Brioche dough
   (page 51)
Egg wash (page 15)
1 tablespoon sesame seeds

TO ASSEMBLE
12 bacon rashers
12 eggs
1 jar Tomato kasundi (page 205)

Once you have proved the dough, you will need to shape and bake your buns (see also images on page 53).

Line two baking trays with baking paper. Tip the dough onto a lightly floured kitchen bench and divide it into twelve equal pieces, about 55 g (2 oz) each.

First, knock out any large bubbles in each piece of dough. The dough is now ready to be shaped into balls. To do this, place your dominant hand over a piece of dough and push it down as you move your hand in a circular motion, rotating the dough in your palm. Applying pressure as you shape the bun builds strength in the dough and makes it more taut. This should take about 30 seconds. Repeat with the remaining dough pieces, placing them on the lined trays about 6 cm (2½ in) apart.

Loosely cover the tray with plastic wrap and prove at 22–24°C (72–75°F) for 1 hour, or until risen by half. Preheat the oven to 170°C (340°F) about 40 minutes into the final prove. Pour about 150 g (5½ oz) water into a tray at the bottom of the oven.

After an hour, check the buns – they should wobble slightly when you shake the tray. Test the buns by gently pressing the surface. If your fingertip leaves a dent, they're ready to bake, but if the dough springs back quickly, they need more time.

Lightly brush the buns with egg wash and sprinkle with sesame seeds. Bake for 12–14 minutes, turning and swapping the trays and removing the water tray halfway through. The buns should be a deep golden colour and smell incredible. Transfer to a wire rack to cool for 10 minutes.

Meanwhile, cook the bacon and fry the eggs. Slice each bun in half horizontally. Spread a generous spoonful of tomato kasundi over the bases, then layer with a rasher of bacon and a fried egg. Finish with the bun tops.

PEAR AND BLACK PUDDING BREAKFAST GALETTES

MAKES 6

The pastry we use for these galettes is really versatile and easy to work with. It's great for both sweet and savoury dishes for lunch and dinner, and now we're using it to make breakfast as well!

To make life easier, prepare the pastry and kale chips the night before, then you just have to slice the pear and black pudding, assemble the galettes and crack some eggs to finish them off. The trick is timing it so the egg is cooked until just runny enough, but it's still much easier than poaching eggs. The combination of pear, black pudding and egg is warming and fills you up for the day ahead. The kale chips contribute texture and a bit of virtue.

Put the pastry on a lightly floured kitchen bench and divide it into six equal pieces. Roll each piece into a disc 3 mm (⅛ in) thick – they will be 19–20 cm in diameter – and lightly score a circle 3 cm (1¼ in) in from the edge. Cover and put in the fridge for at least 30 minutes, or until you're ready to make the galettes.

Preheat the oven to 110°C (230°F). Trim the kale and cut the hard stems out of the leaves, keeping as many leaves whole as possible. Toss the leaves in a bowl with the olive oil and vinegar to coat, rubbing the dressing into each leaf. Lay the kale on a baking tray and bake for 12 minutes, then turn the leaves over and bake for a further 6–8 minutes until crispy. Set aside to cool.

Meanwhile, slice the pears into slivers about 5 mm (¼ in) thick. The exact shape is not important, as the pear will sit at the bottom of the galette. Remove the pips. Slice the black pudding into discs about 3 mm (⅛ in) thick.

Remove the pastry discs from the fridge and place them on sheets of baking paper. Lay the pear slices over each in a circle that meets the border you marked on the pastry. You want the pear to fill the crust of the galette once it's folded over, leaving a hole in the middle to crack the egg into later. Arrange the black pudding in a circle over the top of the pear, again meeting the border and leaving a well in the middle for the egg.

Fold the margin of pastry in towards the centre, over the edge of the filling, and then crimp the pastry edges together. Lightly brush the exposed pastry border with egg wash and sprinkle with fennel seeds, if using.

Return the galettes to the fridge. Turn the oven up to 190°C (375°F). To get the bottom of the pastries nicely browned and cooked through, put two baking trays in the oven to heat up, or use a pizza stone if you have one.

1 quantity Rye flaky shortcrust pastry (page 36)
½ bunch curly kale
20 g (¾ oz/1 tablespoon) olive oil
10 g (⅓ oz/2 teaspoons) apple-cider vinegar
3 medium pears
2 black puddings (approx. 400 g/14 oz)
Egg wash (page 15)
1 tablespoon fennel seeds (optional)
6 medium eggs, at room temperature
verjuice or lemon juice, to finish
fine salt
freshly ground black pepper

Slide the galettes on the baking paper onto the hot trays. Bake for 10 minutes, then reduce the oven to 180°C (360°F) and turn and swap the trays. Bake for a further 15 minutes, or until the pastry is cooked and just starting to become golden. Take the trays out of the oven (or slide out your oven shelf) and break one egg into the middle of each galette. Be careful not to break the yolk or spill the white over the edges. Return to the oven for a further 6–8 minutes, or until the eggs are just set, with a slight wobble indicating runny yolks. Transfer to a wire rack to cool for a few minutes.

Place the galettes onto plates. Drizzle with a little verjuice, scatter over the kale chips and season to taste with a little salt and pepper.

KIMCHI AND CHEDDAR PUFF PASTRY TARTS
MAKES 8

MAKE IT GLUTEN-FREE
Use gluten-free flaky pastry

Our friend Jihee makes the best kimchi I've ever tasted. She uses beautiful organic cabbage, which she leaves in large pieces instead of shredding it to mush. The texture adds so much to the joy of eating it.

I often make these tarts because we always have a jar of kimchi and some cheddar in the fridge. They only use a few ingredients, so it's really worthwhile seeking out good-quality kimchi and cheddar. Or try them with sauerkraut instead of kimchi.

———

Put the pastry on a lightly floured kitchen bench and roll it out into a rectangle measuring 40 × 50 cm (15¾ × 19¾ in) and 4 mm (⅛ in) thick. Cut out eight rectangles, 18 × 12 cm (7 × 4¾ in) – there should be enough pastry left over on each side to tidy up the edges. Lay the pastry between two sheets of baking paper and put it in the fridge to rest for 20 minutes.

Preheat the oven to 190°C (375°F). Line two large baking trays with baking paper. Heat a chargrill or griddle pan over a medium heat and dry-fry the spring onion halves to give a bit of char on all sides. Remove from the pan and set aside to cool.

Remove the pastry rectangles from the fridge. Use a fork to prick the centre of each rectangle a few times, leaving a 2 cm (¾ in) border all around. Lightly brush the borders with egg wash, then divide the kimchi between the tarts, laying it in the centre. Top with two pieces of grilled spring onion and a few slices of cheese, overlapping the slices. Sprinkle the borders with sesame seeds.

Bake for 10 minutes, or until the pastry borders start to rise around the filling, then reduce the oven to 180°C (360°F) and turn and swap the trays. Bake for a further 8–10 minutes until the pastry is golden and flaky. Transfer to a wire rack to cool for a few minutes. Scatter some sliced spring onion over the top and serve warm.

1 quantity Puff pastry (page 32)
8 spring onions (scallions), trimmed and halved, plus 1 spring onion, sliced, to garnish
Egg wash (page 15)
560 g (1 lb 4 oz) kimchi
240 g (8½ oz) cheddar, sliced
1 tablespoon sesame seeds

BUCKWHEAT ENGLISH MUFFINS

MAKES 8

MAKE IT VEGAN
Use oil instead of butter

This recipe is inspired by and adapted from Dan Lepard's muffin recipe in one of my favourite baking books, *The Handmade Loaf*. Being sourdough muffins, they have great depth of flavour and will last well for several days.

English muffins are an excellent vessel for all things brunch. A well-made muffin has lots of holes to perfectly capture the runny egg and hollandaise from your Benedict – yum. The dough is cooked on both sides in a hot pan, then sliced in half and toasted. I love the flavour and texture the buckwheat brings to this version – earthy, warming, and perfect with just a smear of cultured butter on top. Rolled oats can be successfully substituted for a softer flavour.

I use my Lodge pan to cook the muffins. It's a heavy cast-iron pan with a fitted lid, ideal for this recipe. A large heavy-based frying pan with a lid will also work, but you may need to cook the muffins for longer, as the pan won't retain as much heat as a cast-iron one.

Preheat the oven to 160°C (320°F). Spread the buckwheat groats onto a baking tray and toast in the oven for 20 minutes, or until they're a light tan colour. Cool completely, then lightly crush them using a mortar and pestle or with a rolling pin. Transfer to a small bowl and add the boiling water. Set aside to soften for 10 minutes, then drain.

Combine the softened buckwheat, flour, warm water, sourdough starter, vinegar and salt in a large bowl. Mix well with your hands, gently massaging the ingredients together to remove any lumps. The dough should be quite sticky. Pour in the melted butter, then use your hands to work the butter into the dough until it becomes one mass. If you find it easier, tip the dough onto a lightly floured kitchen bench and knead it for a few minutes. Cover the bowl with a damp tea towel (dish towel) and rest for 30 minutes.

The dough is now ready to be folded. Give the dough a set of folds every 30 minutes for the first 2 hours. To fold, wet your hands, then use one hand to hold the bowl and the other to fold. Grab a piece of dough on the side of the bowl, then pull and stretch it up and over the middle to the other side of the bowl. Repeat this six to eight times, moving around the edge of the bowl. Cover and rest the dough between each set of folds.

After the last set of folds, cover and rest the dough in a warm place for 3 hours. Ideally the temperature should be around 22–24°C (72–75°F). If the room is too cold, put the dough in your (cold) oven with the light on, with a tray of hot water at the bottom to create

Ingredients

- 50 g (1¾ oz) buckwheat groats
- 80 g (2¾ oz) boiling water
- 350 g (12½ oz) bakers (strong) flour, plus extra for dusting
- 180 g (6½ oz) warm water at 26°C (79°F)
- 120 g (4½ oz) liquid sourdough starter (see pages 18 and 143)
- 40 g (1½ oz/2 tablespoons) apple-cider vinegar
- 7 g (¼ oz/1 heaped teaspoon) fine salt
- 30 g (1 oz/1½ tablespoons) melted unsalted butter

warmth and humidity. The dough is ready when you see that it is gassy and bubbly with air pockets – it should wobble a little if you gently shake the bowl. You should be able to stretch the dough between your fingers.

Gently tip the dough onto a lightly floured kitchen bench. Use a sieve to lightly and evenly dust the top of the dough as well. Ease the dough gently with your fingers into a rectangle roughly measuring 20 × 28 cm (8 × 11 in) and 3 cm (1¼ in) thick. You want to minimise any air loss in the dough, so work with a light touch. Cut out six circles using an 8 cm (3¼ in) round cutter. Gather all the trimmings together, fold the dough over itself and then gently flatten and cut out two more circles. These last two muffins will be slightly denser than the others because you will have knocked some air out, but they'll be just as tasty. Or, to save time, cut the dough into six or eight rectangles.

If you want to cook your muffins the next day, cover with a damp tea towel and place in the fridge. When you are ready to bake, let them come up to room temperature and finish proving as below.

To prove your muffins, leave them in a warm place covered with a damp tea towel, or again put them in the oven to prove. The proving time is variable and depends on the temperature of the room: if it's cool, let them prove longer; if it's warm, you will be able to bake sooner. As a guide, it should take 1½–2 hours if the temperature is around 22–24°C (72–75°F). They will rise by half and will wobble slightly if you shake the tray. Test the dough by gently pressing the surface. If your fingertip leaves a dent, they're ready to bake, but if the dough springs back quickly, cover them again and give them more time.

To cook the muffins, heat your cast-iron pan over a medium heat for 20 minutes so you have good radiant heat. Using a dough scraper or spatula, gently place two or three muffins at a time in the hot pan, leaving space between them, as they will spread and rise in the pan. (You might like to do a test-run first with just one muffin, to check the heat of the pan and how long it takes to cook. Once cool, open it up to see if it's fully cooked inside, then make a note of the cooking time.)

Cook with the lid on over a medium–low heat for 8–10 minutes on each side. You are looking for an even golden crust, so check the first batch after a few minutes to make sure it's not browning too quickly. If it cooks too quickly, it will be too dark on the outside and the crumb will be underbaked and doughy; if it cooks too slowly, it will dry out.

Repeat for the rest of the muffins, transferring them to a wire rack to cool. The muffins keep well for a few days fresh, or can be frozen, then cut in half and toasted as needed.

Pictured on page 68.

HAM AND CHEESE PALMIERS

MAKES 20

EASY TO ADAPT
MAKE IT GLUTEN-FREE
Use gluten-free flaky pastry and mustard

This is a much quicker version of the classic ham and cheese croissant. I love the combination of ham and cheese wrapped in rich pastry first thing in the morning. These palmiers fit the bill and are visually impressive to boot, puffing into beautifully caramelised love hearts in the oven. They are a firm favourite with everyone in our family.

Unless you are catering for a crowd, this recipe will provide more than you can eat in one sitting. I like to make a full batch and freeze some for a quick bake later. They will last for one month in the freezer.

Put the pastry on a lightly floured kitchen bench and roll it out into a rectangle measuring 36 × 45 cm (14¼ × 17¾ in) and 4 mm (⅛ in) thick. Lay the pastry so that one long side is parallel with the edge of the bench.

On one short side, mark four notches along the edge of the pastry, starting from the bottom: at 8.5 cm (3¼ in), 17 cm (6¾ in), 19 cm (7½ in) and 27.5 cm (11 in). You will use these notches as a guide for filling and folding the palmiers.

Spread the mustard evenly over the pastry, avoiding the 2 cm (¾ in) strip between the middle two notches. Lay the ham over the pastry in two strips – one strip between the first and second notches and another strip between the third and fourth notches. Use half the ham for each strip. Lay the cheese directly over the ham, again using half for each strip.

Lift up the bottom section of the pastry nearest you and fold it over the ham and cheese to meet the notch at 17 cm (6¾ in), then lightly brush with egg wash. Fold the top section down to meet the notch at 19 cm (7½ in) and repeat the brushing. Both strips of filling should now be covered in pastry, leaving a 2 cm (¾ in) gap in the middle. Next, fold the top half down over the bottom half, using the 2 cm (¾ in) gap as a hinge.

Brush the exposed pastry with egg wash and sprinkle generously with sesame seeds. Gently turn the roll over and repeat on the other side, so the entire exposed surface of the pastry is well coated with seeds. Put the roll on a tray and refrigerate for 30 minutes to firm up the pastry – it will be easier to cut when chilled.

Line a large tray with baking paper. Use a sharp knife to trim the edges of the pastry roll, then cut 2 cm (¾ in) slices through the cross-section of the pastry. Transfer the slices to the lined tray, taking care they don't unravel. Chill for at least 30 minutes before baking. At this stage, you can wrap and freeze them until needed.

1 quantity Puff pastry (page 32)
40 g (1½ oz/2 tablespoons)
    Wholegrain mustard (page 211)
200 g (7 oz) sliced ham
150 g (5½ oz) gruyère, thinly
    sliced
Egg wash (page 15)
60 g (2 oz) sesame seeds

To bake the palmiers, preheat the oven to 190°C (375°F). Line as many baking trays with baking paper as required to fit the palmiers – space them 5 cm (2 in) apart so they can expand during baking.

Bake for 10 minutes, then reduce the oven to 180°C (360°F). Bake for a further 14–16 minutes, turning and swapping the trays halfway through, until the palmiers are golden and puffed to a lovely heart shape. Transfer to a wire rack to cool for 10 minutes, then eat on the same day.

Pictured on page 69.

SPRING ONION AND CHEDDAR SCONES
MAKES 8-10

'Oh yum! Cheddar scones are my favourite!' says young Clover. She loves using different cookie cutters to make a variety of shapes, especially the unicorn one. Simple to make and delicious, these are perfect for younger members of the family who love to bake.

This recipe relies on the combination of flour, liquid, baking powder, salt and fat (in this case, butter) for the scones' structure, and they will rise better when baked chilled or frozen. Once the fat is frozen into the dough, it stays solid for longer, holding the structure as it bakes and rises. By the time the flour and liquid have developed and set the crumb, the fat eventually melts, leaving layers or air pockets where the solid fat was, creating a delicate flaky scone.

———

Cut the chilled butter into 1 cm (½ in) dice and return it to the fridge to get really cold while you weigh up the rest of your ingredients.

Line a baking tray with baking paper. Put the flour, baking powder, bicarbonate of soda and salt in a large bowl and whisk to combine, removing any large lumps. Tip the dry ingredients onto the kitchen bench and scatter over the chilled butter cubes. Use a rolling pin to break the butter into the flour, gathering the flour in with a dough scraper or spatula as you go, until the mixture is crumbly with shards of butter the size of rolled oats still visible. These small pieces of butter are important for the structure and texture of the baked scone, so be careful not to overmix at this stage. Return the mixture to the bowl, add the spring onion and 220 g (8 oz) of the grated cheese and toss to combine.

In a separate bowl, lightly whisk together the eggs and sour cream. Make a well in the centre of the dry ingredients and pour the egg mixture into it. Use a knife or a dough scraper to cut the flour into the wet mixture until you have an even crumble texture. Tip the mixture onto a lightly floured bench and use your hands to bring it together into a firm dough, handling it as little as possible so you don't melt the butter pieces or overwork the gluten in the flour.

Roll the dough into a slab roughly measuring 20 × 28 cm (8 × 11 in) and 3 cm (1¼ in) thick. Trim the edges, then cut the dough into eight

220 g (8 oz) unsalted butter, chilled

500 g (1 lb 2 oz) plain (all-purpose) flour

12 g (½ oz/2 teaspoons) baking powder

3 g (¹⁄₁₀ oz/½ teaspoon) bicarbonate of soda (baking soda)

12 g (½ oz/2 teaspoons) fine salt

6 spring onions (scallions), trimmed and sliced 3–4 mm (⅛ in) thick

280 g (10 oz) cheddar, grated

100 g (3½ oz/2 medium) eggs, at room temperature

240 g (8½ oz) sour cream or buttermilk

50 g (1¾ oz/2½ tablespoons) cream or full-cream (whole) milk

rectangles. Gather up the trimmings and push them together, then cut out another scone or two. Place the scones, evenly spaced, on the lined tray. Cover loosely with a tea towel (dish towel) and refrigerate for a couple of hours or freeze for 30 minutes, to set the butter back into the dough. At this stage, you can wrap and freeze the scones for up to 1 month.

To bake the scones, preheat the oven to 180°C (360°F). Gently warm the cream if necessary, to bring it to a slightly runny consistency. Lightly brush the scones with cream and sprinkle with the remaining 60 g (2 oz) cheese. Put the tray on the top oven shelf and bake for 18 minutes, then turn the tray and bake for a further 2–3 minutes until golden. Transfer to a wire rack to cool for a couple of minutes, then eat on the same day.

CELERIAC, KALE AND HAZELNUT MUFFINS
MAKES 6

These muffins take me back to when I worked as a chef in a two-Michelin-star restaurant in London, circa 1998. We used to serve an appetiser of celeriac purée with crisp toasted hazelnuts. These rich, earthy flavours are such a winning combination.

I've used wholemeal flour here, as I love the flavour of whole grains in my baking, but feel free to try different flours – khorasan or spelt are delicious and will work just as well.

Use this recipe as a base and change out the flavours depending on what's in season. Instead of celeriac, try roasting apple and parsnip together, or change it up completely with roasted parsnip, chicory and mustard with a touch of honey.

300 g (10½ oz) celeriac
30 g (1 oz/1½ tablespoons) olive oil
25 g (1 oz) curly kale
40 g (1½ oz) toasted hazelnuts
75 g (2¾ oz) plain (all-purpose) flour
75 g (2¾ oz) wholemeal (whole-wheat) flour
6 g (⅕ oz/1 teaspoon) baking powder
3 g (¹⁄₁₀ oz/½ teaspoon) fine salt
50 g (1¾ oz/1 medium) egg, at room temperature
150 g (5½ oz) milk kefir
100 g (3½ oz) unsalted butter, melted
grated zest of 1 lemon

Roast the celeriac ahead of time so it has time to cool. Preheat the oven to 200°C (390°F). Peel the celeriac and roughly chop into 1 cm (½ in) dice. Toss in a roasting tray with 20 g (¾ oz/1 tablespoon) of the olive oil, then roast for 25 minutes, or until starting to colour. Set aside to cool completely.

To make the muffins, preheat the oven to 190°C (375°F) and grease six holes of a standard muffin tin with a little butter (you can also use patty pans/cupcake liners if you like).

Trim the kale and cut the hard stems out of the leaves, then roughly chop the leaves. Roughly chop the hazelnuts, reserving some whole for the topping. Combine the celeriac, kale and chopped hazelnuts in a bowl.

Put the flours, baking powder and salt in a medium bowl and whisk to combine, removing any lumps in the flour. In a separate large bowl, whisk together the egg, milk kefir, melted butter, lemon zest and remaining 10 g (⅓ oz/2 teaspoons) olive oil. Fold the flour mixture into the milk mixture until well combined. Add the celeriac mixture and stir with a spoon until evenly distributed through the batter.

Divide the mixture between the muffin holes and top each muffin with a few whole hazelnuts. Bake for 15 minutes, then turn the tin and bake for a further 5–10 minutes until starting to colour on top. Leave in the tin for 5 minutes, then turn out on a wire rack to cool.

NETTLE AND GRUYÈRE MUFFINS
MAKES 6

I started using nettles in cooking after we received some soil for our raised gardens beds, which then produced a prodigious amount of nettles several months later. Being curious, I gloved up and harvested them. Now I use nettles for risottos, soups and many different bakes. They're rich in nutritional value and have a gentler, fresher flavour than other dark leafy greens. Nettles do take a bit of determination to tackle — so wear gloves when handling them raw to avoid being stung. Spinach, or any other green that's not too woody, would be a suitable alternative. Simply chop any larger leaves.

If you like to spice things up a bit, add about 50 g (1¾ oz) sliced fresh chilli or pickled jalapeños to the batter.

Preheat the oven to 190°C (375°F) and grease six holes of a standard muffin tin with a little butter (you can also use patty pans/cupcake liners if you like).

Put the flours, baking powder and salt in a medium bowl and whisk to combine, removing any lumps in the flour. In a separate large bowl, whisk together the egg, milk, melted butter and lemon zest. In a third bowl, combine 120 g (4½ oz) of the cheese with the nettles. Fold the flour mixture into the milk mixture until well combined. Add the cheese and nettle mixture and stir with a spoon until well distributed through the batter.

Divide the mixture between the muffin holes. Sprinkle the remaining 30 g (1 oz) cheese over the top. Bake for 10 minutes, then reduce the oven to 180°C (360°F) and turn the tin. Bake for a further 12–15 minutes until golden. Leave in the tin for 5 minutes, then turn out on a wire rack to cool.

100 g (3½ oz) plain (all-purpose) flour
90 g (3 oz) wholemeal (whole-wheat) flour
6 g (⅕ oz/1 teaspoon) baking powder
3 g (¹⁄₁₀ oz/½ teaspoon) fine salt
50 g (1¾ oz/1 medium) egg, at room temperature
250 g (9 oz) full-cream (whole) milk
100 g (3½ oz) unsalted butter, melted
grated zest of 1 lemon
150 g (5½ oz) gruyère, grated
90 g (3 oz) stinging nettle leaves

BACON AND ONION QUICHE

SERVES 8-10

EASY TO ADAPT
MAKE IT GLUTEN-FREE
Use gluten-free flaky pastry

This is my version of a quiche lorraine, the classic French savoury tart. Quiche can be a bit divisive, with as many people professing to loving it as hating it. Personally, I think this mostly reflects the variability in quality – quiche is one of those things that is easy to make badly. A great quiche relies on good ingredients and knowing and trusting your oven. The result is satisfying, versatile and easily transportable, and it is well worth the effort learning to perfect this bake.

I like to make and blind bake the shell in advance. Once you've lined the tin with pastry, chill it in the fridge before baking to produce a flakier crust. I blind bake with aluminium foil for good heat distribution and so you get right into the corners, and I like to use sugar because it's cheap and provides an even weight as the pastry bakes. If there are any cracks in the pastry after blind baking, seal them by brushing a little egg wash over them before filling the quiche. For larger holes or tears, use some excess pastry to fill the gap and brush with egg wash, then return to the oven for a few minutes. Once baked, the shell will keep for up to four days at room temperature in an airtight container.

First line your tart tin (see also page 18). Lightly grease a 23 cm (9 in) round, 3.5 cm (1½ in) deep tart tin with a little butter. Put the pastry on a lightly floured kitchen bench and roll it out into a large disc 3–4 mm (⅛ in) thick. Gently lay the pastry over the tin, then use your thumb to press the pastry firmly into the base. Trim off the excess pastry with a knife, leaving a little overhanging the edge to allow for shrinkage. Transfer to the fridge to rest for 1 hour.

Preheat the oven to 190°C (375°F). Line the rested pastry case with aluminium foil and fill with granulated sugar until heaped. Bake for 30 minutes, then reduce the oven to 160°C (320°F), remove the foil and sugar and bake for a further 20 minutes, or until golden. If you find the middle puffs up, prick the pastry a few times with a fork.

To prepare the custard, whisk together the eggs, cream and milk in a large bowl. Add the thyme, salt and pepper and whisk them through. Add the cheese and stir to evenly distribute it.

To bake the quiche, preheat the oven to 190°C (375°F). Meanwhile, heat a frying pan over a medium heat and fry the bacon until crispy. Remove from the pan and cool, then roughly chop.

Spread a thin layer of caramelised onion over the base of the tart shell. Evenly distribute the bacon pieces over the top.

½ quantity Flaky shortcrust pastry (page 36)
granulated sugar or baking weights, for blind baking
250 g (9 oz/5 medium) eggs
250 g (9 oz) cream
250 g (9 oz) full-cream (whole) milk
1 tablespoon chopped thyme
1 teaspoon fine salt
½ teaspoon freshly ground black pepper
130 g (4½ oz) gruyère, grated
180 g (6½ oz) streaky bacon
100 g (3½ oz) Caramelised onions (page 209)

Give the custard a stir to evenly disperse the ingredients, then transfer it to a jug to make filling the quiche easier. Slide out your oven shelf, place the tin on the shelf, then pour the custard into the shell, being careful not to overfill it. Alternatively, fill it on the bench and carefully transfer to the oven.

Bake for 10 minutes, then reduce the oven to 160°C (320°F). Bake for a further 30–35 minutes, turning the tin halfway through, until the centre of the quiche feels firm but still has a slight wobble. It should be firm rather than runny, but only just cooked. Transfer to a wire rack and cool in the tin for at least 30 minutes to let the custard set. Serve warm or at room temperature. Keeps in the fridge for 3–4 days.

CKLED

USHROOM

LEEKS

MIDDAY

13 LUNCHTIME FAVOURITES
PAGES 82-109

MIDDAY

Simple pies and sausage rolls, nourishing quiches and more ... these are the staples of the local bakery, but better. Take your own baking to work, a weekend picnic or just enjoy it at home.

My version of the classic beef pie is drawn from my days at Sydney's Bourke Street Bakery, where it was always a bestseller no matter what was on the menu or whether it was 4°C or 40°C outside.

The Cornish equivalent from my childhood is, of course, the pasty. Originally made to take down the mines, the pasty was held in soot-blackened hands by the crimped edge so as not to spoil the rest. I'm breaking from tradition here with a cheese and onion version, and a steak and stilton one. Both are portable, delicious and guaranteed to sustain you until dinnertime.

For an occasion requiring cutlery, try the tomato and anchovy spelt galette or the pickled mushroom and macadamia tart, enjoyed with a glass of something delicious.

STEAK AND STILTON PASTIES
MAKES 8

MAKE IT GLUTEN-FREE
Use gluten-free flaky pastry

I don't usually diverge from a traditional Cornish pasty. The subject of variations in pasty fillings is a tricky one for a Cornish person, as we are a patriotic lot. Even with so many options available now, most people I know are staunch traditionalists. But I've asked around and found a few who will admit that a steak and stilton pasty is acceptable. And, when pushed, they even agreed that it's delicious. This combination works so well; the blue cheese and steak are perfectly balanced to make you savour every bite.

If you're proper Cornish, use a good Cornish blue cheese, but other cheeses will work too – a nice bitey cheddar or even parmesan will taste great.

———

Peel and roughly chop the onions. Scrub and roughly chop the potatoes. Cut the leek into 1 cm (½ in) slices. Don't worry about perfectly diced veg here – the housewives of Cornwall never did. Cut the beef into 1 cm (½ in) dice.

Combine the vegetables, beef and thyme in a large bowl. Don't season the mix until you are about to assemble the pasties. This is to avoid the salt drawing water out of the ingredients and creating a wet mess – you want that moisture to come out during the baking, to create gravy inside the pasty.

Line two baking trays with baking paper. Put the pastry on a lightly floured kitchen bench and cut it into eight equal pieces, about 160 g (5½ oz) each. Roll each piece into a disc 20–22 cm (8–8¾ in) in diameter and 4 mm (⅛ in) thick – don't worry about getting perfect circles.

Add the salt and pepper to the beef mixture and mix thoroughly. Divide the filling between the pasty rounds – roughly 200 g (7 oz) of filling for each – placing it on the top half of each pastry disc, leaving a 2 cm (¾ in) border around the top edge for crimping. Crumble 40 g (1½ oz) of the blue cheese over the filling.

Lightly brush the pastry border at the top with egg wash, then fold the bottom half of the pastry over the filling so that it meets the pastry on the other side. Push out any air pockets and cup your hands over the top to bring it all together tightly. Crimp the edges together with your thumb and forefinger to form a rope-like seam along the side of the pasty. Patch any holes with a little dampened

400 g (14 oz) onions
280 g (10 oz) old floury potatoes, such as desiree, sebago, maris piper or king edwards
280 g (10 oz) leeks, white and green parts
800 g (1 lb 12 oz) skirt or chuck steak
1 tablespoon chopped thyme
1 quantity Lard shortcrust pastry (page 38)
18 g (⅔ oz/3 teaspoons) fine salt
6 g (⅕ oz/2 teaspoons) freshly ground black pepper
320 g (11½ oz) stilton or other blue cheese
Egg wash (page 15)

rolled-out pastry. As you finish each pasty, place it on the lined trays, leaving a 5 cm (2 in) gap between them so they bake evenly. Lightly brush the top of the pasties with egg wash, then cut a slit in the tops to allow the steam to vent while baking. Put in the fridge to cool, or freeze some to bake another day.

To bake the pasties, preheat the oven to 190°C (375°F). Bake for 10 minutes, then reduce the oven to 160°C (320°F). Bake for a further 50 minutes, turning and swapping the trays halfway through, until golden brown. Transfer to a wire rack to cool. The filling will be very hot, so let them rest for at least 10 minutes before eating.

GREENS, FETA AND RICOTTA HAND PIES
MAKES 6

These wonderful parcels of healthy greens wrapped in golden puff pastry are based on the famous Greek dish spanakopita, a filo pastry pie filled with spinach, feta and ricotta. You can make these pies with any greens you like – kale, spinach or silverbeet all work well. I like to use Warrigal greens, an Australian native spinach, but I will happily use any dark leafy green that is available at the time.

———

1 quantity Puff pastry (page 32)
500 g (1 lb 2 oz) mixed dark leafy greens
20 g (¾ oz/1 tablespoon) olive oil
4 spring onions (scallions), trimmed and thinly sliced
2 garlic cloves, finely chopped
2 medium eggs
200 g (7 oz) sheep's milk feta
200 g (7 oz) full-fat ricotta
50 g (1¾ oz) toasted pine nuts
10 g (⅓ oz) chopped dill
grated zest and juice of 1 lemon
1½ teaspoons fine salt
¼ teaspoon freshly ground black pepper
Egg wash (page 15)

Put the pastry on a lightly floured kitchen bench and roll it out into a rectangle roughly measuring 38 cm × 56 cm (15 × 22 in) and 4 mm (⅛ in) thick. Cut out six 18 cm (7 in) discs. Lay the pastry discs between two sheets of baking paper and refrigerate until you are ready to assemble.

Wash the leafy greens and drain well. If using a variety of greens, divide them into groups and plan to cook each type separately; for example, English spinach will cook more quickly than say kale or rainbow chard leaves. Heat the olive oil in a large frying pan over a medium heat. Add the greens, in batches to avoid overcrowding the pan, and cook until just wilted (don't overcook them – they will cook further in the oven). As each batch is cooked, transfer it to a colander over the sink. Lightly squeeze out any excess water to prevent the pastry from becoming soggy during the bake.

Once cool, roughly chop the greens and put them in a large bowl. Add the spring onion, garlic, eggs, feta, ricotta, pine nuts, dill, lemon zest and juice, salt and pepper. Use your hands or a spoon to thoroughly mix everything together.

Lay the pastry discs on a floured bench and lightly roll each one into an oval shape. Divide the filling between the pastry ovals, placing it on the top half of the oval, leaving a 2 cm (¾ in) border around the top edge. Push down on the greens to create a compact dome shape. Lightly brush the pastry border at the top with egg wash, then fold the bottom half of the pastry over the filling so that it meets the pastry on the other side. Push out any air pockets and press the edges of the pastry together to seal the pies. Lightly brush the tops with egg wash, then use a blunt knife to score a leaf-shaped pattern over the top. Be careful not to cut through the pastry. Put in the fridge until you are ready to bake, or freeze them and bake when required.

Preheat the oven to 190°C (375°F). Line two baking trays with baking paper. Put the pies on the lined trays and bake for 15 minutes, then turn and swap the trays. Bake for a further 15 minutes, or until the pastry is golden and flaky. Transfer to a wire rack to cool for 10 minutes before serving.

CHICKEN, SWEET CORN AND BASIL PIE

SERVES 6

We ate at Liam Tomlin's restaurant Banc in Sydney back at the turn of the century and had a wonderful appetiser with sweet corn and basil. The combination blew me away – it was so simple and effective. I love using basil in dishes: with tomatoes, bacon, avocado, eggs and in salads. And everybody loves sweet corn, right? So, this is a very flavoursome pie and a real winner.

Slice the kernels off the corn cobs and set aside. Chop the chicken into 2 cm (¾ in) dice.

Heat 20 g (¾ oz/1 tablespoon) of the olive oil in a large heavy-based frying pan over a medium–high heat. Brown the chicken in batches, adding more oil as required. Remove from the pan and set aside.

Return the pan to a medium heat and melt 30 g (1 oz) of the butter with a splash of olive oil. Add the onion and garlic and cook with the lid on, stirring occasionally, for 5 minutes, or until softened. Stir in the corn, chicken, wine, salt and pepper. Cook with the lid on, stirring occasionally, for 10–15 minutes until the chicken is cooked through. Set aside to cool with the lid off.

To make a béchamel, warm the milk in a small saucepan over a low heat until it just comes to a simmer, then remove the pan from the heat. Melt the remaining 60 g (2 oz) butter in a large saucepan over a medium heat. Add the flour and whisk to combine. Cook, whisking, for 4–5 minutes until the mixture darkens slightly and resembles sand. Add the warm milk in three stages, whisking after each addition to get rid of any lumps. Bring to a simmer for a few minutes until the sauce thickens. Add the parmesan and stir it through until well combined.

Add the chicken mixture to the béchamel and stir to combine thoroughly. Stir in the basil. Once it's cooled a little, check the seasoning, adding more salt and pepper, to taste. Refrigerate for a few hours or overnight before assembling and baking your pie(s) (see page 22).

3 corn cobs
600 g (1 lb 5 oz/approx. 4) boneless, skinless chicken thighs
60–80 g (2–2¾ oz) olive oil
90 g (3 oz) unsalted butter
3 medium onions
2 garlic cloves
100 g (3½ oz) white wine
1 teaspoon fine salt
¼ teaspoon freshly ground black pepper
300 g (10½ oz) full-cream (whole) milk
60 g (2 oz) plain (all-purpose) flour
60 g (2 oz) parmesan, grated
30 g (1 oz) basil leaves
pastry of choice (see Pie basics, page 22)

CHEESE AND ONION PASTIES
MAKES 8

These are super easy to make. When I'm looking for an alternative to a Cornish pasty, this cheese and onion combination is definitely my favourite. The vegetables cook in the melted cheese within the pastry, so when you cut the pasty open, you get this wonderfully gooey filling oozing out.

I like the extra onion piquancy that the chives bring; parsley will also work well, but it will be a bit softer in flavour. To make these suitable for vegetarians, use butter in place of lard in the pastry.

———

500 g (1 lb 2 oz) cheddar,
  coarsely grated
500 g (1 lb 2 oz) onions,
  roughly chopped
480 g (1 lb 1 oz) potatoes,
  scrubbed and roughly
  chopped
2 garlic cloves, thinly sliced
20 g (¾ oz/1 tablespoon)
  snipped chives
9 g (⅓ oz/1½ teaspoons) fine salt
5 g (⅕ oz/2 teaspoons) freshly
  ground black pepper
1 quantity Wholemeal lard
  shortcrust pastry (page 38)
Egg wash (page 15)

Put the cheese, onion, potato, garlic, chives, salt and pepper in a large bowl and mix well. Set aside while you prepare the pastry.

Line two baking trays with baking paper. Put the pastry on a lightly floured kitchen bench and cut it into eight equal pieces, about 160 g (5½ oz) each. Roll each piece into a disc 20–22 cm (8–8¾ in) in diameter and 4 mm (⅛ in) thick – don't worry about getting perfect circles.

Divide the cheese and onion mixture between the pasty rounds – roughly 190 g (6½ oz) of filling for each – placing it on the top half of each pastry disc, leaving a 2 cm (¾ in) border around the top edge for crimping.

Lightly brush the pastry border at the top with egg wash, then fold the bottom half of the pastry over the filling so that it meets the pastry on the other side. Push out any air pockets and cup your hands over the top to bring it all together tightly. Crimp the edges together with your thumb and forefinger to form a rope-like seam along the side of the pasty. Patch any holes with a little dampened, rolled-out pastry. As you finish each pasty, place it on the lined trays, leaving a 5 cm (2 in) gap between them so they bake evenly. Lightly brush the top of the pasties with egg wash, then cut a slit in the tops to allow the steam to vent while baking. Put in the fridge to cool, or freeze some to bake another day.

To bake the pasties, preheat the oven to 190°C (375°F). Bake for 10 minutes, then reduce the oven to 160°C (320°F). Bake for a further 50 minutes, turning and swapping the trays halfway through, until golden brown. Transfer to a wire rack to cool. The filling will be very hot, so let them rest for at least 10 minutes before eating.

PICKLED MUSHROOM AND MACADAMIA TARTS

MAKES 6

EASY TO ADAPT
MAKE IT VEGAN
Use vegan flaky pastry, plant-based milk and vegan cheese

This is a variation of a very popular dish we made at Tivoli Road Bakery. The base of the tarts is filled with a deliciously rich macadamia cream and then topped with pickled mushrooms. The recipe makes more macadamia cream than you'll need, but it's hard to successfully blitz a smaller quantity of cream in most food processors, so I recommend making the full amount. Use the leftover cream in other dishes – with salads, crudités, or as a base for roasted vegetables for a simple midweek dinner.

I've used a variety of mushrooms here to enhance the textures in the dish. I like oyster, shiitake and shimeji, but use whatever is local and in season. And finish it off with a shaving of hard sheep's or goat's milk cheese. An aged cheese is perfect – something with a bit of bite that adds umami. For a vegan version, grate some macadamia over the top instead.

These tarts make a good light lunch, or size down for a canape. They're a great option when entertaining because the components can be prepared in advance, then quickly assembled just before serving.

————

To make the pickled mushrooms, combine the mushrooms and shallot in a heatproof bowl. Bring the white-wine vinegar and water to the boil in a small saucepan, then pour the hot pickling liquid over the mushrooms and shallot. Cover and set aside for 2 hours.

Strain the mushroom mixture, reserving 20 g (¾ oz/1 tablespoon) of the pickling liquid, and transfer to a medium bowl. Put the reserved pickling liquid in a small bowl with the mustard, olive oil, salt and pepper and stir to combine well. Pour the dressing over the mushrooms, add the herbs and stir to combine.

To make the macadamia cream, preheat the oven to 170°C (340°F). Put the macadamias on a baking tray and toast for 5 minutes, or until starting to colour, then remove from the tray and set aside to cool. Put the cooled nuts, macadamia oil, apple-cider vinegar, milk and water in a food processor and blitz for 7–10 minutes until smooth. Season to taste with salt.

Put the pastry on a lightly floured kitchen bench and roll it out 4 mm (⅛ in) thick. Cut out six 15 cm (6 in) circles. Reuse pastry scraps to make more circles. Lay the pastry between two sheets of baking paper and put in the fridge to rest for 20 minutes.

Preheat the oven to 190°C (375°F). Line two large baking trays with baking paper. Remove the pastry circles from the fridge. Use a fork to prick the centre of each circle a few times, leaving a 2 cm (¾ in) border all around. Lightly brush the borders with egg wash. Bake for

PICKLED MUSHROOMS
250 g (9 oz) mixed mushrooms, sliced or torn
2 shallots, thinly sliced
75 g (2¾ oz) white-wine vinegar
75 g (2¾ oz) water
3 g (⅒ oz/½ teaspoon) dijon or Wholegrain mustard (page 211)
40 g (1½ oz/2 tablespoons) olive oil
½ teaspoon fine salt
¼ teaspoon freshly ground black pepper
1 tablespoon chopped parsley
1 tablespoon snipped chives

MACADAMIA CREAM
200 g (7 oz) macadamia nuts
30 g (1 oz/1½ tablespoons) macadamia oil
15 g (½ oz/3 teaspoons) apple-cider vinegar
130 g (4½ oz) full-cream (whole) milk
90 g (3 oz) water
fine salt, to taste

PASTRY

1 quantity Gluten-free flaky
  pastry (pastry 48)
Egg wash (page 15)

TO ASSEMBLE

100 g (3½ oz) hard, aged sheep's
  or goat's milk cheese
bitter leaves and edible flowers,
  to garnish

10 minutes, then reduce the oven to 180°C (360°F). Bake for a further
5–6 minutes, turning and swapping the trays halfway through, until
starting to colour. Transfer to a wire rack to cool completely.

To assemble the tarts, place a generous spoonful of macadamia
cream in the middle of each pastry circle, then gently spread it out
to nearly meet the border. Divide the pickled mushrooms between
the tarts, building them up a little on top of the macadamia cream.
Grate the cheese over the top of each tart to finish. Serve with a
bitter leaf salad and edible flowers.

The pictured tart was made using vegan flaky pastry.

PORK, SAGE AND ONION SAUSAGE ROLLS
MAKES 8

EASY TO ADAPT
MAKE IT GLUTEN-FREE
Use gluten-free flaky pastry and breadcrumbs

This is my favourite sausage roll. Onion and sage are classic pairings with pork and this is a great rendition – I could eat them for breakfast, lunch and dinner. I use really good mince from the shoulder and flavour it generously with herbs. If you have a choice, opt for coarsely ground mince. It's great for a sausage roll because you get a nice distribution of fat all the way through. This stops the mince from drying out and gives the sausage roll more flavour.

Heat the olive oil in a medium frying pan over a medium heat. Add the onion and garlic and cook with the lid on, stirring occasionally, for 10 minutes, or until lightly caramelised. Stir in the sage, rosemary, thyme and salt, then transfer to a large bowl to cool.

Add the pork and breadcrumbs to the onion mixture. Use clean hands or a wooden spoon to mix thoroughly until all the elements are evenly distributed through the mince. Transfer the mixture into a large piping bag with a 3 cm (1¼ in) diameter hole. (A piping bag will make it easier to distribute the filling, but you can always spoon it onto the pastry if you don't have one.) Refrigerate while you prepare the pastry.

Line a large baking tray with baking paper. Put the pastry on a lightly floured kitchen bench and roll it out into a rectangle measuring 30 × 60 cm (12 × 23½ in) and 4 mm (⅛ in) thick. Lay the pastry so that one long side is parallel with the edge of the bench. Cut the pastry in half lengthways so you have two sheets, 15 × 60 cm (6 × 23½ in).

Pipe half the filling in a horizontal line one-third of the way up each pastry sheet. Brush the pastry above each line of filling with egg wash. Lift up the pastry along the edge closest to you and fold it up and over the filling. Seal the pastry along the egg-washed edge, so the seam sits underneath the filling. The pastry should hold the filling evenly and not be too tight.

Brush the tops and sides of both rolls with egg wash, lightly pierce along the top with a fork, then sprinkle with mustard seeds. Cut each roll into 15 cm (6 in) logs (or, as pictured, cut them into 5 cm/ 2 in lengths to make party snacks; it should make around 24). Lay your sausage rolls on the lined tray and rest them in the fridge for 30 minutes. At this stage, you can freeze them until required.

To bake the sausage rolls, preheat the oven to 190°C (375°F). Bake from cold for 10 minutes, then reduce the oven to 180°C (360°F). Bake for a further 25–30 minutes (reduce by 10 minutes for mini rolls), turning the tray halfway through, until the pastry is golden, puffed and flaky. Transfer to a wire rack to cool for 10 minutes before eating.

60 g (2 oz) olive oil
4 medium onions, finely chopped
4 garlic cloves, finely chopped
2 tablespoons finely chopped sage
1 tablespoon finely chopped rosemary
1 tablespoon finely chopped thyme
1½ teaspoons fine salt
1 kg (2 lb 4 oz) minced (ground) pork
100 g (3½ oz) coarse dry breadcrumbs
1 quantity Puff pastry (page 32)
Egg wash (page 15)
1 tablespoon yellow mustard seeds

EASY TO ADAPT
MAKE IT GLUTEN-FREE
Use gluten-free flaky pastry

MAKE IT VEGAN
Use vegan flaky pastry, vegan cheese and plant-based milk for brushing, omit anchovies

TOMATO AND ANCHOVY SPELT GALETTES
MAKES 6

Based on the Mediterranean classic, pissaladière, these simple, moreish galettes are bursting with flavour. Most of the ingredients are pantry staples, so it's a great weekend lunch or weeknight hero, but my favourite time and place to eat this is during a picnic on a warm summer's day, sitting under a tree.

I've used cherry tomatoes here, but you can use larger tomatoes if you prefer – just make sure they're at their peak of seasonal juicy sweetness.

———

1 quantity Wholemeal spelt flaky shortcrust pastry (page 36)
300 g (10½ oz) Caramelised onions (page 209)
30 g (1 oz) anchovy fillets
120 g (4½ oz) cherry tomatoes, halved
60 g (2 oz) olives, pitted and halved
1 tablespoon oregano or thyme leaves
Egg wash (page 15)
60 g (2 oz) parmesan (optional)
herbs, to garnish (optional)

Put the pastry on a lightly floured kitchen bench and divide it into six equal pieces. Roll each piece into a disc 3 mm (⅛ in) thick and 16 cm (6¼ in) in diameter and lightly score a circle 2 cm (¾ in) in from the edge. Cover and refrigerate for at least 30 minutes, or until you're ready to make the galettes.

Remove the pastry discs from the fridge and place them on sheets of baking paper. Spoon about 50 g (1¾ oz) of caramelised onion onto each galette base and spread it out to meet the 2 cm (¾ in) margin. Divide the anchovy fillets between the galettes, then top with the tomatoes, olives and herbs. Fold the margin of pastry in towards the centre, over the edge of the filling, then crimp the pastry edges together to contain the filling. Lightly brush the exposed pastry border with egg wash.

Return the galettes to the fridge while you preheat the oven to 190°C (375°F). To get the bottom of the pastries nicely browned and cooked through, put two baking trays in the oven to heat up, or use a pizza stone if you have one.

Slide the galettes on the baking paper onto the hot trays. Bake for 10 minutes, then reduce the oven to 180°C (360°F) and turn and swap the trays. Bake for a further 18–20 minutes until the pastry edges are deep golden brown. Transfer to a wire rack to cool for a few minutes, then use a vegetable peeler to shave a little parmesan over each galette, if using, and garnish with herbs if desired. Serve with a leafy salad.

QUINOA AND SWEET POTATO SAUSAGE ROLLS
MAKES 8

MAKE IT GLUTEN-FREE
Use gluten-free flaky pastry and breadcrumbs

These sausage rolls, filled with lots of good-for-you veggies, pulses, grains and seeds, are great for children who aren't so fond of their veggies – our young one certainly loves them! And it's a great recipe for getting them involved, too – picking the herbs, peeling the carrot and sweet potato, or brushing the egg wash over the pastry.

———

Cook the quinoa and lentils (you can do this ahead of time). Put the lentils in a medium saucepan and cover generously with water. Bring to the boil, then simmer for 15–18 minutes until tender. Rinse the quinoa in cold water, then put it in a small saucepan with 160 g (5½ oz) water. Bring to the boil, then cover with the lid and reduce the heat to low for 15 minutes until the water has been absorbed.

Heat the olive oil in a large, deep frying pan over a medium heat. Add the onion, carrot, sweet potato, celery and garlic. Cook with the lid on, stirring occasionally, for 8–10 minutes until softened. Add the ground cumin and cinnamon for the last minute or so, to bring out the fragrance.

Add all the vegetables to the quinoa and lentils. Add the parmesan, breadcrumbs, herbs, tomato paste, lemon juice, salt and pepper. Stir to combine well, then set aside to cool. Mix through the egg to bind everything together. Transfer the mixture into a large piping bag with a 3 cm (1¼ in) diameter hole. (A piping bag will make it easier to distribute the filling, but you can always spoon it onto the pastry if you don't have one.) Refrigerate while you prepare the pastry.

Line a large baking tray with baking paper. Put the pastry on a lightly floured kitchen bench and roll it out into a rectangle measuring 30 × 60 cm (12 × 23½ in) and 4 mm (⅛ in) thick. Lay the pastry so that one long side is parallel with the edge of the bench. Cut the pastry in half lengthways so you have two sheets, 15 × 60 cm (6 × 23½ in).

Pipe half the filling in a horizontal line one-third of the way up each pastry sheet. Brush the pastry above each line of filling with egg wash. Lift up the pastry along the edge closest to you and fold it up and over the filling. Seal the pastry along the egg-washed edge, so the seam sits underneath the filling. The pastry should hold the filling evenly and not be too tight.

Brush the tops and sides of both rolls with egg wash, lightly pierce along the top with a fork, then sprinkle with cumin seeds. Cut each roll into 15 cm (6 in) logs. Lay your sausage rolls on the lined tray and rest them in the fridge for 30 minutes. At this stage, you can freeze them until required.

80 g (2¾ oz) quinoa
180 g (6½ oz) du Puy lentils
60 g (2 oz) olive oil
1 large onion, finely chopped
1 large carrot, finely chopped
1 sweet potato (approx. 250 g/ 9 oz), finely chopped
1 large celery stalk, finely chopped
4 garlic cloves, finely chopped
2 teaspoons ground cumin
2 teaspoons ground cinnamon
140 g (5 oz) parmesan, coarsely grated
80 g (2¾ oz) coarse dry breadcrumbs
20 g (¾ oz) chopped coriander (cilantro) leaves
20 g (¾ oz) chopped parsley
40 g (1½ oz/2 tablespoons) tomato paste (concentrated purée)
juice of 1 lemon
1½ teaspoons fine salt
2 teaspoons freshly ground black pepper
3 medium eggs, lightly beaten
1 quantity Puff pastry (page 32)
Egg wash (page 15)
1 tablespoon cumin seeds

To bake the sausage rolls, preheat the oven to 190°C (375°F). Bake from cold for 10 minutes, then reduce the oven to 180°C (360°F). Bake for a further 25–30 minutes, turning the tray halfway through, until the pastry is golden, puffed and flaky. Transfer to a wire rack to cool for 10 minutes before eating.

SMOKED TROUT, FENNEL AND NASTURTIUM CAPER QUICHE

SERVES 8-10

EASY TO ADAPT
MAKE IT GLUTEN-FREE
Use gluten-free flaky pastry

I can't emphasise enough that once you have mastered quiche pastry and the custard mix, the possibilities are endless. I've made versions of this quiche with smoked eel instead of the trout, cooked or raw beetroot instead of fennel, and freshly grated horseradish in place of capers.

———

First line your tart tin (see page 18). Lightly grease a 23 cm (9 in) round, 3.5 cm (1½ in) deep tart tin with a little butter. Put the pastry on a lightly floured kitchen bench and roll it out into a large disc 3–4 mm (⅛ in) thick. Gently lay the pastry over the tin, then use your thumb to firmly press the pastry into the base. Trim off the excess pastry with a knife, leaving a little overhanging the edge to allow for shrinkage. Transfer to the fridge to rest for 1 hour.

Preheat the oven to 190°C (375°F). Line the rested pastry case with aluminium foil and fill with granulated sugar until heaped. Bake for 30 minutes, then reduce the oven to 160°C (320°F), remove the foil and sugar and bake for a further 20 minutes, or until golden. If you find the middle puffs up, prick the pastry a few times with a fork.

To prepare the custard, whisk together the eggs, cream and milk in a large bowl. Add the thyme, salt and pepper and whisk them through.

Turn the oven back up to 190°C (375°F). Melt the butter in a frying pan over a medium heat. Add the fennel and shallot and cook, stirring frequently, for 10–12 minutes until softened and starting to colour. Add the garlic and cook for 1 minute, or until fragrant. Remove from the heat and set aside.

Spread a layer of the fennel mixture over the base of the tart shell. Evenly distribute the smoked trout, kale and nasturtium capers over the top.

Give the custard a stir to evenly disperse the ingredients, then transfer it to a jug to make filling the quiche easier. Slide out your oven shelf, place the tin on the shelf, then pour the custard into the shell, being careful not to overfill it. Or fill it on the bench and carefully transfer to the oven.

Bake for 10 minutes, then reduce the oven to 160°C (320°F). Bake for a further 30–35 minutes, turning the tin halfway through, until the centre of the quiche feels firm but still has a slight wobble. It should be firm rather than runny, but only just cooked. Transfer to a wire rack and cool in the tin for at least 30 minutes to let the custard set. Serve warm or at room temperature. Keeps in the fridge for 3–4 days.

The pictured quiche was made using rye flaky shortcrust pastry.

½ quantity Flaky shortcrust pastry (page 36)
granulated sugar or baking weights, for blind baking
250 g (9 oz/5 medium) eggs
240 g (8½ oz) cream or crème fraîche
240 g (8½ oz) full-cream (whole) milk
1 tablespoon chopped thyme
1 teaspoon fine salt
½ teaspoon freshly ground black pepper
40 g (1½ oz) unsalted butter
1 small fennel bulb (approx. 250 g/9 oz), thinly sliced
2 shallots (approx. 80 g/2¾ oz), thinly sliced
2 garlic cloves, finely chopped
1 small hot-smoked trout, in small chunks (150 g/5½ oz picked)
2 curly kale leaves, tough stems removed and leaves chopped
15 g (½ oz) Nasturtium capers, roughly chopped (page 210)

MUSHROOM, RED ONION AND TARRAGON QUICHE

SERVES 8-10

EASY TO ADAPT
MAKE IT GLUTEN-FREE
Use gluten-free flaky pastry

I love the sweetness of roasted red onion with the earthiness of mushrooms, and they both work so well with the tarragon. For variation in flavour and texture, I use different types of mushrooms, but you can use your favourite mushrooms or whatever is in season.

I've used crème fraîche in this recipe to add a little acid; you could use sour cream or a plain milk kefir instead. Fresh goat's cheese provides a balance for the sweetness of the roasted onions – a more mature cheese will give a deeper flavour.

———

First line your tart tin (see page 18). Lightly grease a 23 cm (9 in) round, 3.5 cm (1½ in) deep tart tin with a little butter. Put the pastry on a lightly floured kitchen bench and roll it out into a large disc 3–4 mm (⅛ in) thick. Gently lay the pastry over the tin, then use your thumb to firmly press the pastry into the base. Trim off the excess pastry with a knife, leaving a little overhanging the edge to allow for shrinkage. Transfer to the fridge to rest for 1 hour.

Preheat the oven to 190°C (375°F). Line the rested pastry case with aluminium foil and fill with granulated sugar until heaped. Bake for 30 minutes, then reduce the oven to 160°C (320°F), remove the foil and sugar and bake for a further 20 minutes, or until golden. If you find the middle puffs up, prick the pastry a few times with a fork.

Cut the onions in half or thirds (depending on size), leaving the skin on. Trim the top and bottom of each onion so it sits flat, then put the pieces, cut side up, in a roasting tin. Drizzle with 30 g (1 oz/1½ tablespoons) of the olive oil and sprinkle the thyme and nigella seeds over the top. Divide 30 g (1 oz) of the butter into small pieces and place on top of each onion piece. Roast for 45 minutes, or until the onion is softened and slightly browned on the edges. Set aside to cool.

Use a pastry brush to remove any dirt from the mushrooms, then slice or shred into 3–4 cm (1¼–1½ in) pieces. Melt 20 g (¾ oz) butter with 20 g (¾ oz/1 tablespoon) olive oil in a large frying pan over a medium heat. Add half the mushrooms and half the garlic and cook, stirring, until golden brown. Add a squeeze of lemon juice to the pan, then transfer the mushrooms to a colander to drain. Repeat with the remaining mushrooms, garlic and lemon juice, adding more oil and butter as required.

½ quantity Flaky shortcrust pastry (page 36)
granulated sugar or baking weights, for blind baking
3 medium red onions
70 g (2½ oz) olive oil
1 tablespoon chopped thyme
10 g (⅓ oz/2 teaspoons) nigella seeds
70 g (2½ oz) unsalted butter
250 g (9 oz) mixed mushrooms
2 garlic cloves, thinly sliced
grated zest and juice of 1 lemon
250 g (9 oz/5 medium) eggs
240 g (8½ oz) crème fraîche
240 g (8½ oz) full-cream (whole) milk
1½ teaspoons fine salt
½ teaspoon freshly ground black pepper
1 tablespoon chopped tarragon
80 g (2¾ oz) soft goat's cheese

To prepare the custard, whisk together the eggs, crème fraîche, milk, salt, pepper, lemon zest and tarragon in a large bowl.

Turn the oven back up to 190°C (375°F). Squeeze out any remaining moisture from the mushrooms and scatter them over the base of the tart shell. Remove the skins from the onion halves, then pat off any excess moisture with a clean tea towel (dish towel). Put one onion half, cut side up, in the middle of the quiche, then arrange the remaining onions in a circle around it. Break up the goat's cheese and scatter it over the mushrooms and in between the onions.

Give the custard a stir to evenly disperse the ingredients, then transfer it to a jug to make filling the quiche easier. Slide out your oven shelf, place the tin on the shelf, then pour the custard into the shell, being careful not to overfill it. Or fill it on the bench and carefully transfer to the oven. The custard should fill the spaces around the onions, leaving them visible at the top.

Bake for 10 minutes, then reduce the oven to 160°C (320°F). Bake for a further 20–25 minutes, turning the tin halfway through, until the centre of the quiche feels firm but still has a slight wobble. It should be firm rather than runny, but only just cooked. Transfer to a wire rack and cool in the tin for at least 30 minutes to let the custard set. Serve warm or at room temperature. Keeps in the fridge for 3–4 days.

Pictured on page 104. The quiche was made using wholemeal flaky shortcrust pastry.

RATATOUILLE AND BOCCONCINI PIE
SERVES 8

EASY TO ADAPT
MAKE IT VEGAN
Use vegan flaky pastry, use oil instead of butter, use vegan cheese

This is my take on ratatouille, the classic French Provençal vegetable dish originally from Nice. It features a wonderful variety of vegetables, plus I've added bocconcini to marry it all together and bring out the best of summer. The great thing about this pie is its versatility: use mozzarella instead of bocconcini, take out or add any vegetable you prefer, stick with just one colour of capsicum or mix up the colours and eat the rainbow! You just need to ensure that your total vegetable weight is similar to the recipe.

———

Start by prepping all your vegetables so that the cooking process flows nicely. Trim and chop the eggplant, zucchini and capsicums into 2–3 cm (¾–1¼ in) pieces, discarding the membranes and seeds from the capsicums. Peel and slice the onions. Peel and thinly slice the garlic.

Heat 20 g (¾ oz/1 tablespoon) of the olive oil in a large frying pan over a medium–high heat. Working in batches, cook the eggplant, zucchini and capsicum for 4–5 minutes, adding more oil as required. Stop cooking before the vegetables get soft; you just want a bit of colour at this stage. Transfer each batch of vegetables into a large bowl.

Meanwhile, melt the butter with 20 g (¾ oz/1 tablespoon) olive oil in a large heavy-based saucepan over a medium heat. Cook the onion and garlic, stirring, for 10–12 minutes until starting to soften and caramelise. Add the tomatoes and bring to a simmer, then stir in the balsamic vinegar, salt and pepper. Add all the fried vegetables, then reduce the heat to low and cook just under a simmer for 20 minutes, or until the vegetables are softened and everything comes together. Remove the pan from the heat and stir in the lemon zest, basil and thyme. Once it's cooled a little, check the seasoning, adding more salt and pepper, to taste. Refrigerate for a few hours or overnight.

To assemble and bake your pies, follow the instructions on page 22. If making one pie, scatter the bocconcini halves over the ratatouille filling before adding the pastry lid. If making individual pies, use two bocconcini halves for each pie. I like to sprinkle pepitas over the pastry top before baking. Serve with a leafy summer salad.

The pies pictured on page 105 were made using savoury shortcrust pastry for the base and plain puff pastry for the tops.

500 g (1 lb 2 oz) eggplant (aubergine)
400 g (14 oz) zucchini (courgettes)
800 g (1 lb 12 oz) capsicums (bell peppers)
2 large onions
6 garlic cloves
100–150 g (3½–5½ oz) olive oil
20 g (¾ oz) unsalted butter
1 × 400 g (14 oz) tin whole tomatoes or 6 large ripe tomatoes, roughly chopped
20 g (¾ oz/1 tablespoon) balsamic vinegar
1½ teaspoons fine salt
½ teaspoon freshly ground black pepper
grated zest of 1 lemon
40 g (1½ oz/1 small bunch) basil, leaves picked and torn
1 tablespoon chopped thyme
pastry of choice (see Pie basics, page 22)
8 bocconcini, cut in half
pepitas (pumpkin seeds), for sprinkling

PEA, ASPARAGUS AND SOUR CREAM QUICHE
SERVES 8–10

Asparagus is a reason in itself to enjoy seasonal eating. The appearance of the first spears heralds the arrival of spring and warmer days to come. In our house, the first ones are eaten very lightly steamed with no other adornment, but as the season progresses we start to think of different ways to cook with them.

Eat this quiche outdoors in the sunshine, preferably with a chilled glass of dry sherry and the feeling of grass between your toes.

½ quantity Flaky shortcrust pastry (page 36)
granulated sugar or baking weights, for blind baking
250 g (9 oz/5 medium) eggs
240 g (8½ oz) sour cream
240 g (8½ oz) full-cream (whole) milk
grated zest of 1 lemon
2 tablespoons snipped chives
1½ teaspoons fine salt
½ teaspoon freshly ground black pepper
100 g (3½ oz) parmesan, coarsely grated
20 g (¾ oz/1 tablespoon) olive oil
12 asparagus spears (approx. 150 g/5½ oz), trimmed
100 g (3½ oz) fresh peas
1 handful pea shoots, leaves and flowers

First line your tart tin (see page 18). Lightly grease a 23 cm (9 in) round, 3.5 cm (1½ in) deep tart tin with a little butter. Put the pastry on a lightly floured kitchen bench and roll it out into a large disc 3–4 mm (⅛ in) thick. Gently lay the pastry over the tin, then use your thumb to firmly press the pastry into the base. Trim off the excess pastry with a knife, leaving a little overhanging the edge to allow for shrinkage. Transfer to the fridge to rest for 1 hour.

Preheat the oven to 190°C (375°F). Line the rested pastry case with aluminium foil and fill with granulated sugar until heaped. Bake for 30 minutes, then reduce the oven to 160°C (320°F), remove the foil and sugar and bake for a further 20 minutes, or until golden. If you find the middle puffs up, prick the pastry a few times with a fork.

To prepare the custard, whisk together the eggs, sour cream and milk in a large bowl. Add the lemon zest, chives, salt and pepper and whisk them through. Add the parmesan and stir to evenly distribute it.

Turn the oven back up to 190°C (375°F). Meanwhile, heat the olive oil in a chargrill or griddle pan over a medium–high heat. Grill the asparagus to slightly colour on all sides. Set aside to cool, then chop into 2–3 cm (¾–1¼ in) pieces. Scatter the asparagus, peas, pea shoots, leaves and flowers over the base of the tart shell.

Give the custard a stir to evenly disperse the ingredients, then transfer it to a jug to make filling the quiche easier. Slide out your oven shelf, place the tin on the shelf, then pour the custard into the shell, being careful not to overfill it. Or fill it on the bench and carefully transfer to the oven.

Bake for 10 minutes, then reduce the oven to 160°C (320°F). Bake for a further 30–35 minutes, turning the tin halfway through, until the centre of the quiche feels firm but still has a slight wobble. It should be firm rather than runny, but only just cooked. Transfer to a wire rack and cool in the tin for at least 30 minutes to let the custard set. Serve warm or at room temperature. Keeps in the fridge for 3–4 days.

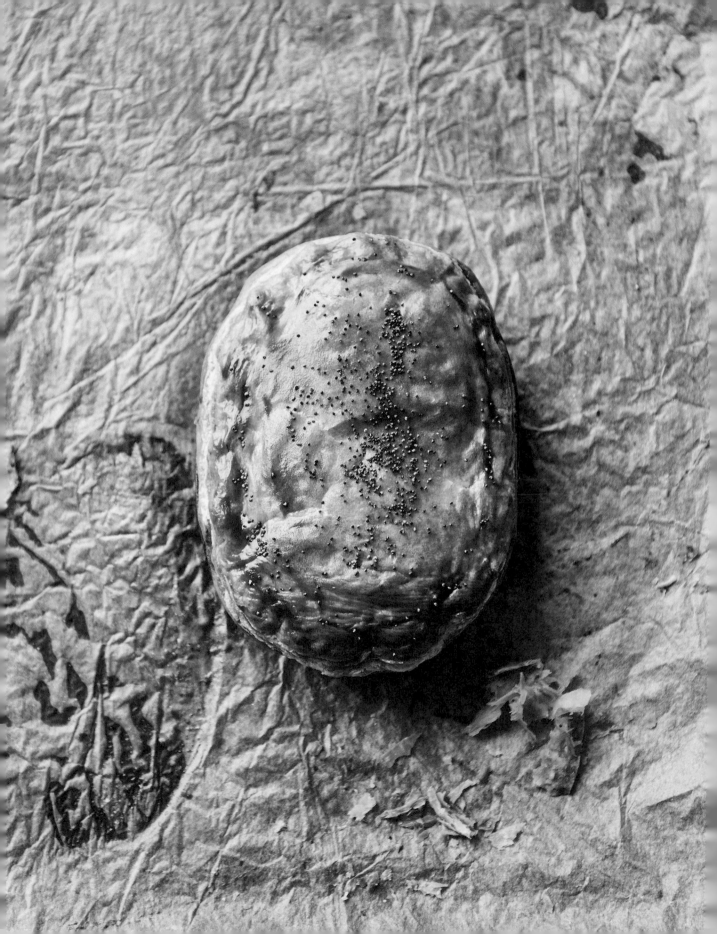

STEAK AND VEGEMITE PIE
SERVES 6

This riff on the ubiquitous Australian bakery classic uses Vegemite to bring saltiness and some yeasty umami to the pie. Top tip: Vegemite is a great addition to stocks and braises; I have even used it in desperation to make a stock cube more flavoursome. But remember, a little goes a long way – just like on your toast!

In the initial braise of the beef, you want to take it to the point where it's no longer tough, but no further than that. Remember that it will cool in the liquid and then go back in the oven once it's in the pie case, so it will have a chance to cook more later.

———

100 g (3½ oz) olive oil
2 medium onions, roughly
    chopped
2 large carrots, roughly chopped
3 medium celery stalks, chopped
4 garlic cloves, chopped
1 tablespoon thyme
800 g (1 lb 12 oz) chuck or skirt
    steak, cut into 2 cm (¾ in)
    cubes
1 × 400 g (14 oz) tin whole
    peeled tomatoes
60 g (2 oz) malt vinegar
9 g (⅓ oz/1½ teaspoons) fine salt
1 teaspoon freshly ground black
    pepper
1 teaspoon Vegemite or Marmite
5 g (⅕ oz/1 teaspoon) potato
    starch
10 g (⅓ oz/2 teaspoons) water
pastry of choice (see Pie basics,
    page 22)

Heat 50 g (1¾ oz/2½ tablespoons) of the olive oil in a large heavy-based saucepan or cast-iron casserole dish over a low heat. Add the onion, carrot, celery, garlic and thyme and cook with the lid on, stirring occasionally, for 8–10 minutes until softened.

Meanwhile, heat the remaining 50 g (1¾ oz/2½ tablespoons) olive oil in a large heavy-based frying pan over a medium–high heat. Brown the beef in batches and set aside.

Add the tomatoes, vinegar, salt and pepper and Vegemite to the veggies, then add the browned beef. Use water (or beef stock or red wine if you have it) to rinse out the tomato tin and to deglaze the frying pan you cooked the beef in, pouring the water into the pan with the vegetables and beef until the meat is just covered – roughly three tins' worth. Stir to combine. Bring to the boil, then reduce the heat to low and simmer for about 2 hours, or until the beef is tender but not mushy. Check the pan frequently and skim any scum or oil off the top.

Strain the cooked beef mixture into a colander set over a bowl, reserving the liquid. Return the liquid to the pan and reduce it over a high heat until you have about 500 g (1 lb 2 oz) left.

Combine the potato starch and water, then whisk it into the liquid in the pan. Add the beef and vegetables, stirring to combine. Remove the pan from the heat. Once it's cooled a little, check the seasoning, adding more salt and pepper, to taste. Refrigerate for a few hours or overnight before assembling and baking your pie(s) (see page 22).

The pictured pie was made using savoury shortcrust pastry for the base and plain puff pastry for the top. The pie was garnished with poppy seeds.

GRUYÈRE

ALL DAY

14 BAKES FOR ANY TIME, ANYWHERE
PAGES 112-145

WHOLEGRA

MUSTARD

ALL DAY

There are some things you could eat at any time – a wholesome loaf, a fresh scone slathered with butter, or cheesy gougères straight from the oven. This chapter covers snacks and comforting bakes that will prop you up in the morning and settle you in the evening, or see you through an afternoon slump.

For me, pork pies are the gold standard of all-day food. They are the ultimate in portable fare – tasty and satisfying without being too big to ruin your appetite.

The quiche shells are made with flaky pastry. I like to keep them crisp, so they are baked a deep golden brown, then filled and enjoyed at any time. I've been making quiche for years and I love the challenge of getting it just right. The custard should be velvety, with enough variation in the filling to create different bursts of texture and flavour with each mouthful. I love that moment when you take it out of the oven and it lands on a cooling rack with a slight wobble in the middle.

The savoury loaves provide a wonderful base for lazy weekend brunches, and are perfect on their own for lunch boxes or an afternoon treat. The scones are universally loved.

Here you'll find a range of bakes that will fill you with goodness, not sweetness. I encourage you to use these recipes and play around with different vegetables, herbs and spices to create your own family favourites.

ASPARAGUS, HAM AND CHEESE BOSTOCKS

MAKES 8

A bostock is a sweet pastry, originally conceived as a way of using up stale brioche. The sliced brioche is softened with a little syrup or jam and spread with frangipane, topped with sliced nuts and baked. Yum.

This version is all savoury, with buttermilk (or any milk) used to soak the brioche, and béchamel standing in for the frangipane. Topped with ham and grilled asparagus, it is ideal for breakfast, lunch or a light supper. It works equally well with sliced tomatoes in summer, or you can add a fried egg to make it more of a croque madame–style dish. These can be made up in advance, then frozen and baked as required.

Lightly grease a 12 × 23 cm (4¾ × 9 in), 7 cm (2¾ in) deep, straight-sided loaf tin. Tip your fully proved brioche dough onto a lightly floured kitchen bench and divide it into three equal pieces, about 220 g (8 oz) each.

You now need to shape each piece of dough into a tight ball. Take one piece and knock out any large bubbles, then fold the outside edges into the middle, and turn it over so the seam is underneath. Place your dominant hand over the dough and push it down as you move your hand in a circular motion, rotating the dough in your palm. You may find it easier to cup both hands around the dough. Applying pressure as you shape the pieces builds strength in the dough and makes it more taut. This process should take about 30 seconds. Repeat with the remaining two pieces. Put the three balls in the tin, smooth side up.

Cover and set aside to prove, ideally at 22–24°C (72–75°F). If the room is too cold, put the dough in your (cold) oven with the light on, with a small tray of hot water at the bottom to create warmth and humidity. As a guide, it should take 1½ hours to prove. After 1 hour, the dough should have risen to almost level with the top of the tin. Once fully proved, the dough should wobble slightly when you shake the tin. Check if it's ready by gently poking the dough. If your fingertip leaves a dent, it's ready, but if the dough springs back quickly, cover again and give it more time.

Preheat the oven to 170°C (340°F). If your dough is ready but your oven is not quite up to temperature, put the tin in the fridge until you are ready to bake. The chilled brioche dough will firm up once chilled, so this will also make it easier to apply the egg wash.

Just before baking, lightly brush the top with egg wash or spray it with water. Bake on the top oven shelf for 25–30 minutes, turning the tin halfway through to ensure an even bake. To test if the loaf is ready, remove it from the tin and tap the bottom; if it sounds hollow

1 quantity Brioche dough (page 51)
Egg wash (page 15) or water spray
400 g (14 oz) buttermilk or milk
16 slices of ham
24 asparagus spears, trimmed and halved
120 g (4½ oz) toasted walnuts, roughly chopped

BÉCHAMEL
500 g (1 lb 2 oz) full-cream (whole) milk
2 cloves
2 whole black peppercorns
50 g (1¾ oz) unsalted butter
50 g (1¾ oz) plain (all-purpose) flour
100 g (3½ oz) gruyère, grated
5 g (⅛ oz/1 teaspoon) Wholegrain mustard (page 211)
1 teaspoon fine salt
¼ teaspoon freshly ground black pepper

it is ready. If not, put it back in the tin and into the oven for a further 5 minutes. If the brioche is underbaked, there will be insufficient structure to hold the loaf up – it will cave in on the sides and collapse.

Leave in the tin for 5 minutes, then turn out onto a wire rack to cool for 30 minutes before using. The kitchen will smell amazing. But, wait! Resist temptation before slicing into the brioche.

To make the béchamel, gently warm the milk, cloves and peppercorns in a small saucepan over a low heat until it just comes to a simmer. Strain the milk into a bowl or jug. Melt the butter in a medium saucepan over a medium heat. Add the flour and whisk to combine. Cook, whisking, for 4–5 minutes until the mixture darkens slightly and resembles sand. Add the infused milk in two stages, whisking after each addition to get rid of any lumps. Bring to a simmer for a few minutes until the sauce thickens. Stir in the cheese, mustard, salt and pepper, then cover the surface with plastic wrap to prevent a skin forming. Set aside until you are ready to assemble.

Preheat the oven to 180°C (360°F). Line a baking tray with baking paper. Cut the brioche loaf into eight slices about 2 cm (¾ in) thick. Put the buttermilk in a wide bowl and very lightly soak the brioche on each side. The brioche should not be completely soaked; you have to be able to handle the slice.

Put the soaked brioche on the lined tray, spacing them evenly apart. Lay two slices of ham over each slice, then divide the béchamel between them, spreading it evenly over the tops and sides. Bake for 16–18 minutes, turning the tray halfway through, until they have a little bit of colour on the sides.

Meanwhile, heat a chargrill or griddle pan over a medium heat. Grill the asparagus for a few minutes on each side. Remove the bostocks from the oven, top each one with grilled asparagus spears, sprinkle with the walnuts and serve.

Pictured on page 118.

POTATO, ASPARAGUS AND GRIBICHE TARTES FINES

MAKES 4

Sauce gribiche is a French classic and one that (I think) is not well known enough. It's basically an egg sauce, but there's a lot going on flavour- and texture-wise. You have the saltiness, acidity and creaminess of the sauce combined with a bit of smokiness from the charred vegetables, creating a dish of piquant deliciousness.

I like the texture of the gluten-free flaky pastry for these tarts, but you can use any of the flaky pastries, or even puff. If you like, bake the pastry rectangles, make the sauce gribiche and boil the potatoes ahead of time. With most of the elements ready to go, assembly is quick and easy whenever you want to serve it.

Adapt this dish to whichever season you're in – replacing the asparagus with mushrooms or baby leeks. Add some cold-smoked salmon or trout for extra decadence.

To make the sauce gribiche, bring a large saucepan of water to the boil. Add the eggs and boil for 10 minutes, then drain and run them under cold water. Peel and roughly chop the eggs or grate on the coarse side of a box grater.

Combine all the remaining gribiche ingredients, except the lemon juice and salt, in a medium bowl. Taste and then season with lemon juice. Do not add salt until you are ready to serve, as the salt may draw out too much moisture and make the sauce runny.

Line a large baking tray with baking paper. Put the pastry on a lightly floured kitchen bench and roll it out into a rectangle measuring 25 × 40 cm (10 × 15¾ in) and 4 mm (⅛ in) thick. Neaten the edges and cut four rectangles, 12 × 18 cm (4¾ × 7 in). Put the rectangles on the lined tray, cover and put in the fridge for 30 minutes.

Preheat the oven to 180°C (360°F). Bake for 18–20 minutes, turning the tray halfway through, until the pastries are golden all over. Transfer to a wire rack to cool.

Meanwhile, wash the potatoes and put them in a medium saucepan of cold water. Bring to the boil over a medium heat, then reduce the heat to low and simmer the potatoes until they are slightly soft, around 20–40 minutes depending on their size and freshness. They're ready when a knife inserted into a potato will go through with little resistance. Drain and set aside to cool. Cut into 5 mm (¼ in) thick slices.

SAUCE GRIBICHE

150 g (5½ oz/3 medium) eggs
55 g (2 oz) round or banana shallots, finely diced
5 g (⅕ oz/1 tablespoon) finely chopped dill
5 g (⅕ oz/1 tablespoon) finely chopped parsley
10 g (⅓ oz) Nasturtium capers, roughly chopped (page 210)
20 g (¾ oz) cornichons, thinly sliced
grated zest of 1 lemon
10 g (⅓ oz/2 teaspoons) Wholegrain mustard (page 211)
55 g (2 oz) crème fraîche
55 g (2 oz) mayonnaise
¼ teaspoon fennel seeds, chopped
¼ teaspoon caraway seeds, chopped
lemon juice, to taste
flaky sea salt, to taste

PASTRY

½ quantity Flaky gluten-free
  pastry (page 48)

TO ASSEMBLE

400 g (14 oz) purple congo,
  kipfler (fingerling) or new
  potatoes
12 asparagus spears, trimmed
8 spring onions (scallions),
  trimmed
flaky sea salt
freshly ground black pepper
olive oil, for drizzling
1 large handful of salad leaves
  and herbs

When you're ready to assemble the pastries, heat a chargrill or
griddle pan over a medium–high heat. Grill the asparagus and spring
onions for 2–3 minutes on each side until lightly charred. Do the
same with the sliced potatoes. Season the veggies with a little salt
and pepper, drizzle with a good splash of olive oil and set aside.
Once cool, cut the asparagus and spring onion into thirds.

Arrange the potato over the base of each pastry rectangle,
overlapping the slices a little. Add the spring onion and asparagus,
then a good spoonful of sauce gribiche. Finish with a few salad
leaves and herbs on top, and a drizzle of olive oil.

Pictured on page 119.

PAPRIKA, CAYENNE AND ROSEMARY CHEESE STRAWS

MAKES 28-30

EASY TO ADAPT
MAKE IT GLUTEN-FREE
Use gluten-free flaky pastry

These cheese straws are a perfect salty snack. Satisfyingly crispy with a smoky umami, they are moreish and addictive. Our daughter just loves them. If you're making them for a spice-sensitive crowd, leave out the cayenne pepper.

I like to make up a batch and freeze them so I can bake off a few for a quick pre-dinner snack or lunch box filler. You can make and bake them all in one go, but you'll need a few large trays, or have to bake them in batches.

Put the pastry on a lightly floured kitchen bench and roll it out into a rectangle measuring 35 × 60 cm (13¾ × 23½ in) and 4 mm (⅛ in) thick. Put the pastry (it's quite long, so loosely roll it if needed) between two sheets of baking paper and refrigerate for 30 minutes.

Lay the pastry on a lightly floured bench with one long side parallel with the edge of the bench. Brush the entire sheet with egg wash. Sprinkle 60 g (2 oz) of the parmesan evenly over the bottom half of the pastry, followed by the rosemary, paprika, cayenne pepper, if using, and salt. Fold the top half of the pastry over the filling and lightly press down over the top to seal. Brush the top with egg wash. Your pastry sheet should now roughly measure 17.5 × 60 cm (7 × 23½ in).

With a large kitchen knife, cut the pastry into vertical strips 2 cm (¾ in) wide. This should yield up to thirty strips. Put the strips on lined trays and refrigerate for at least 30 minutes.

To create the twists, use your fingertips to gently stretch a strip of pastry, starting from the middle and teasing it out towards the ends. Pinch the ends and then rotate them in opposite directions to create lots of twists in the pastry. It should look like rope, about 30 cm (12 in) long. Repeat with all the strips, then return them to the trays and into the fridge to chill. At this stage, you can freeze them until needed.

To bake the straws, preheat the oven to 190°C (375°F). Line a large baking tray with baking paper (if baking them all at once, you'll need two or three large trays). Put the twists on the lined tray, leaving a 4 cm (1½ in) gap between each one, then sprinkle the remaining 40 g (1½ oz) parmesan over the top.

Bake for 10 minutes, then reduce the oven to 180°C (360°F) and turn the tray. Bake for a further 5–6 minutes until golden and flaky. Transfer to a wire rack to cool for 10 minutes, then sprinkle with flaky sea salt. These are best eaten on the day they're baked, but will keep for 2–3 days in an airtight container – refresh them in the oven at 160°C (320°F) for a few minutes.

1 quantity Puff pastry (page 32)
Egg wash (page 15)
100 g (3½ oz) parmesan, finely grated
1 tablespoon chopped rosemary
1½ teaspoons smoked paprika
½ teaspoon cayenne pepper (optional)
½ teaspoon flaky sea salt, plus extra for sprinkling

CHORIZO, RED CAPSICUM AND MANCHEGO QUICHE

SERVES 8-10

EASY TO ADAPT
MAKE IT GLUTEN-FREE
Use gluten-free flaky pastry

This was inspired by my time working at MoVida in Melbourne. My culinary education was definitely along Anglo–French lines, and it was wonderful for me to learn a new way of cooking and flavour combinations.

It used to be hard to come by good chorizo in Australia, but that's changing now, and it's worth seeking out one that is made with quality pork and well seasoned. With great cheese, paprika and a splash of sherry, this combination is one of my favourites. The addition of egg and flaky pastry make for a wonderful breakfast, lunch, or dinner with a glass of sherry.

——

First line your tart tin (see page 18). Lightly grease a 23 cm (9 in) round, 3.5 cm (1½ in) deep tart tin with a little butter. Put the pastry on a lightly floured kitchen bench and roll it out into a large disc 3–4 mm (⅛ in) thick. Gently lay the pastry over the tin, then use your thumb to firmly press the pastry into the base. Trim off the excess pastry with a knife, leaving a little overhanging the edge to allow for shrinkage. Transfer to the fridge to rest for 1 hour.

Preheat the oven to 190°C (375°F). Line the rested pastry case with aluminium foil and fill with granulated sugar until heaped. Bake for 30 minutes, then reduce the oven to 160°C (320°F), remove the foil and sugar and bake for a further 20 minutes, or until golden. If you find the middle puffs up, prick it a few times with a fork.

Heat 50 g (1¾ oz/2½ tablespoons) of the olive oil in a large frying pan over a medium heat. Cook the capsicum, stirring occasionally, for 8–10 minutes until softened and slightly coloured. Add the vinegar and toss the capsicum in it to coat, then transfer to a bowl to cool.

Wipe out the pan and return it to a medium heat. Add the remaining 50 g (1¾ oz/2½ tablespoons) olive oil and fry the spring onion and garlic for 4–5 minutes until softened and slightly coloured. Transfer to the bowl with the capsicum. Reheat the pan again and fry the chorizo on both sides for 5 minutes, or until golden and starting to crisp up. Transfer to the bowl with the capsicum mixture, then stir in the herbs.

To prepare the custard, whisk together the eggs, milk, crème fraîche, salt, pepper and smoked paprika in a large bowl.

Turn the oven back up to 190°C (375°F). Spread the capsicum and chorizo mixture over the base of the tart shell, then sprinkle the cheese over the top.

½ quantity Flaky shortcrust pastry (page 36)
granulated sugar or baking weights, for blind baking
100 g (3½ oz) olive oil
2 red capsicums (bell peppers), thinly sliced, seeds and membranes discarded
20 g (¾ oz/1 tablespoon) sherry vinegar
5 spring onions (scallions), trimmed and thinly sliced
1 garlic clove, finely chopped
2 chorizo (approx. 200 g/7 oz), sliced into 1 cm (½ in) rounds
1 tablespoon chopped rosemary or thyme
250 g (9 oz/5 medium) eggs
240 g (8½ oz) full-cream (whole) milk
240 g (8½ oz) crème fraîche
1½ teaspoons fine salt
½ teaspoon freshly ground black pepper
½ teaspoon smoked paprika
100 g (3½ oz) manchego, coarsely grated

Give the custard a stir to evenly disperse the ingredients, then transfer it to a jug to make filling the quiche easier. Slide out your oven shelf, place the tin on the shelf, then pour the custard into the shell, being very careful not to overfill it. Or fill it on the bench and carefully transfer to the oven.

Bake for 10 minutes, then reduce the oven to 160°C (320°F). Bake for a further 25–30 minutes, turning the tin halfway through, until the centre of the quiche feels firm but still has a slight wobble. It should be firm rather than runny, but only just cooked. Transfer to a wire rack and cool in the tin for at least 30 minutes to let the custard set. Serve warm or at room temperature. Keeps in the fridge for 3–4 days.

RYE SOURDOUGH CRACKERS
MAKES 2 TRAYS

This is a simple but versatile recipe, and if you've been making bread at home, it's a handy way of using up excess sourdough starter. The crackers are great served with cheese, as a canapé base or just as a snack on their own. Once you realise how easy these are to make, you'll never buy an overpriced packet of crackers again.

You can alter the flavour by using different flours; wholemeal or spelt are excellent. And you can make almost endless variations – if using seeds or spices to flavour your crackers, just sprinkle them on top before baking so they toast a little. When flavouring with dried herbs, I prefer to incorporate them into the dough along with the salt and olive oil before mixing. This prevents them burning in the oven. Here are some flavour and serving suggestions for your crackers.

Topping:	Serve with:
za'atar	hummus
nigella seeds	goat's curd and sliced roasted beetroot
dried thyme	baba ganoush
sesame seeds	avocado and furikake
dried rosemary	chicken liver or mushroom pâté

115 g (4 oz) rye flour or wholegrain rye flour

250 g (9 oz) liquid sourdough starter (see pages 18 and 143)

¼ teaspoon flaky sea salt, plus extra for sprinkling

60 g (2 oz) olive oil, plus extra for brushing

1 teaspoon dried herbs, seeds or spices

Combine the flour, sourdough starter, salt, olive oil and herbs, if using, in a medium bowl. Use your hands to mix a dough that is quite firm and dry to touch – it should be similar to a pasta dough or playdough. If the dough is too wet, add a little more flour. If it's too dry, add extra oil, 1 teaspoon at a time. Wrap the dough and put it in the fridge to firm up for at least 30 minutes, or overnight. It will keep for up to 5 days in raw form.

To bake the crackers, preheat the oven to 170°C (340°F). Put the dough on a lightly floured kitchen bench and divide it into two portions (or as many as needed), then roll it into thin sheets about 1 mm (1⁄32 in) thick. To make life really easy, use a pasta machine for this task if you have one.

At this point, you need to decide the form for your crackers. You can bake them in long sheets to be broken up once crisp, or cut them into squares for more precise portions. If you want neat edges, use a knife to trim them or a fluted pastry cutter for a fancy finish.

Line two baking trays with baking paper. Put the dough sheets or squares on the lined trays, lightly brush with olive oil and sprinkle with sea salt and your desired seeds or spices, if using. Bake for about 20 minutes, turning and swapping the trays halfway through, until the crackers start to brown around the edges. Transfer to a wire rack to cool completely. Store for 1 week in an airtight container.

PUMPKIN SCONES

MAKES 8

These scones were inspired by Thanksgiving pumpkin pie. With the natural sweetness from the pumpkin, warming spices and the sharp bite of the parmesan to balance all the flavours, they make for an excellent afternoon treat in the autumn.

This recipe provides an ideal way to use up leftover roasted pumpkin. If you're starting from scratch, make the pumpkin purée a day or so ahead to make it easy to whip up the scones on the day. If you don't have an 8 cm (3¼ in) round cutter, simply cut the scones to your desired size and shape.

———

To make the pumpkin purée, preheat the oven to 190°C (375°F). Cut the pumpkin in half and remove the seeds. Put in a roasting tin, drizzle with the olive oil and season with salt and pepper. Cover with aluminium foil and bake for 1 hour 45 minutes, or until tender. Scoop out the flesh and blitz in a food processor to form a smooth purée. You will need 230 g (8 oz) purée for this recipe.

To make the scones, cut the chilled butter into 1 cm (½ in) cubes and return it to the fridge to get it really cold while you weigh up the rest of your ingredients.

Line a large baking tray with baking paper. Put the flour, baking powder, bicarbonate of soda, salt and spices in a large bowl and whisk to combine, removing any large lumps. Tip the dry ingredients onto the kitchen bench and scatter over the chilled butter cubes. Use a rolling pin to break the butter into the flour, gathering in the flour with a dough scraper or spatula as you roll, until the mixture is crumbly with shards of butter the size of rolled oats still visible. These small pieces of butter are important for the structure and texture of the baked scone, so be careful not to overmix at this stage. Add the coarsely grated parmesan and toss to combine.

Put the pumpkin purée, eggs and milk in a bowl and lightly whisk to combine. Make a well in the centre of the dry ingredients and pour the wet mixture into it. Toss the flour mixture over the liquid and use your hands to gently bring everything together – this may take a minute or two. Use a dough scraper to gather up any loose flour or liquid as you go. Once it is a cohesive mass, roll it out a little and fold it over itself two to three times to help create layers.

PUMPKIN PURÉE

1 small pumpkin (winter squash)
20 g (¾ oz/1 tablespoon) olive oil
fine salt
freshly ground black pepper

SCONES

220 g (8 oz) unsalted butter, chilled
500 g (1 lb 2 oz) plain (all-purpose) flour
12 g (½ oz/2 teaspoons) baking powder
3 g (¹⁄₁₀ oz/½ teaspoon) bicarbonate of soda (baking soda)
12 g (½ oz/2 teaspoons) fine salt
½ teaspoon ground ginger
¼ teaspoon ground cloves
1 teaspoon ground cinnamon
½ teaspoon freshly grated nutmeg
220 g (8 oz) coarsely grated parmesan, plus 50 g (1¾ oz) finely grated, for the topping
230 g (8 oz) pumpkin purée (see above)
100 g (3½ oz/2 medium) eggs, at room temperature
50 g (1¾ oz) full-cream (whole) milk or buttermilk, plus extra, for brushing

Roll the dough into a slab roughly measuring 18 × 28 cm (7 × 11 in) and 3 cm (1¼ in) thick. Use an 8 cm (3¼ in) round cutter to cut out six scones. Gather up the trimmings and push them together, then cut out another scone or two. Place the scones, evenly spaced, on the lined tray. Cover loosely with a tea towel (dish towel) and refrigerate for a couple of hours or freeze for 30 minutes to set the butter back into the dough. At this stage, you can wrap and freeze the scones for up to 1 month.

To bake the scones, preheat the oven to 190°C (375°F). Lightly brush the tops with milk, then sprinkle with the finely grated parmesan. Put the tray on the top oven shelf and bake for 10 minutes, then turn the oven down to 180°C (360°F). Bake for a further 10–12 minutes, turning the tray halfway through, until golden on top. Transfer to a wire rack to cool for a few minutes, then eat on the same day. The flavour of the spices will mellow beautifully as the scones cool.

The finished pumpkin scones are pictured on page 130 (round shape).

RYE, WALNUT AND ANISE MYRTLE SCONES
MAKES 12

These scones are an excellent source of whole grains and nuts, and great for a quick snack or a picnic. I love them as an alternative to crackers to serve with blue cheese, or just slathered with good cultured butter.

The combination of rye and walnut is one that I use often, in everything from brownies to bread. And I love the addition of anise myrtle, an Australian native found in north-eastern New South Wales. The leaves have a strong aniseed scent, and are ground into a powder that gives a wonderful lingering flavour, enhancing the rye even more. You can buy ground anise myrtle online from native food suppliers. If you can't find it, leave it out or substitute with ground aniseed, fennel or star anise.

---

220 g (8 oz) unsalted butter, chilled

200 g (7 oz) rye flour or wholegrain rye flour

300 g (10½ oz) plain (all-purpose) flour

12 g (½ oz/2 teaspoons) baking powder

3 g (⅒ oz/½ teaspoon) bicarbonate of soda (baking soda)

12 g (½ oz/2 teaspoons) fine salt

100 g (3½ oz) toasted walnuts, roughly chopped

¼ teaspoon ground coriander

¼ teaspoon ground cumin

½ teaspoon ground anise myrtle

100 g (3½ oz/2 medium) eggs

260 g (9 oz) sour cream

Egg wash (page 15)

Cut the chilled butter into 1 cm (½ in) dice and return it to the fridge to get it really cold while you weigh up the rest of your ingredients.

Line two baking trays with baking paper. Put the flours, baking powder, bicarbonate of soda and salt in a large bowl and whisk to combine, removing any large lumps. Tip the dry ingredients onto the kitchen bench and scatter over the chilled butter cubes. Use a rolling pin to break the butter into the flour, gathering in the flour with a dough scraper or spatula as you roll, until the mixture is crumbly with shards of butter the size of rolled oats still visible. These small pieces of butter are important for the structure and texture of the baked scone, so be careful not to overmix at this stage. Return to the bowl, add the walnuts, coriander, cumin and anise and mix them through.

In a separate bowl, lightly whisk together the eggs and sour cream. Make a well in the centre of the dry ingredients and pour the egg mixture into it. Use a knife or a dough scraper to cut the flour into the wet mixture until you have an even crumble texture. Tip the mixture onto a lightly floured bench and use your hands to bring it together into a firm dough, handling it as little as possible so you don't melt the butter pieces or overwork the gluten in the flour.

Roll the dough into a slab measuring 20 × 24 cm (8 × 9½ in) and 3 cm (1¼ in) thick, then cut into twelve triangles, 10 cm (4 in) long and 7 cm (2¾ in) wide. Place the scones, evenly spaced, on the lined trays. Cover loosely with a tea towel (dish towel) and refrigerate for a couple of hours or freeze for 30 minutes to set the butter back into the dough. At this stage, you can wrap and freeze the scones for up to 1 month.

To bake the scones, preheat the oven to 180°C (360°F). Lightly brush the tops with egg wash. Bake for 10 minutes, then turn and swap the trays and bake for a further 8 minutes, or until golden on top. Transfer to a wire rack to cool for a few minutes, then eat on the same day.

ZUCCHINI, SPRING ONION AND MILK KEFIR QUICHE

SERVES 8-10

This quiche is all about different flavours and textures. The milk kefir in the custard provides a delightful freshness, and the wholemeal pastry is toothsome and provides an earthy balance. It's studded with sunflower seeds for added texture and enlivened with lemon zest and fresh herbs.

The ingredients for the custard mix are fairly adaptable: use milk instead of milk kefir, or sour cream or crème fraîche for the cream.

———

First line your tart tin (see page 18). Lightly grease a 23 cm (9 in) round, 3.5 cm (1½ in) deep tart tin with a little butter. Put the pastry on a lightly floured kitchen bench and roll it out into a large disc 4 mm (⅛ in) thick. Gently lay the pastry over the tin, then use your thumb to firmly press the pastry into the base. Trim off the excess pastry with a knife, leaving a little overhanging the edge to allow for shrinkage. Transfer to the fridge to rest for 1 hour.

Preheat the oven to 190°C (375°F). Heat a chargrill or griddle pan over a medium heat. Grill the zucchini for 2–3 minutes each side until golden. Transfer to a plate lined with paper towel or a clean tea towel (dish towel) to absorb any excess moisture. Grill the spring onion to give a bit of char on all sides, then add to the zucchini. Set aside to cool.

Line the rested pastry case with aluminium foil and fill with granulated sugar until heaped. Bake for 30 minutes, then reduce the oven to 160°C (320°F), remove the foil and sugar and bake for a further 20 minutes, or until golden. If you find the middle puffs up, prick the pastry a few times with a fork.

To prepare the custard, whisk together the eggs, milk kefir and cream in a large bowl. Add the rosemary, lemon zest, salt and pepper and whisk them through.

Turn the oven back up to 190°C (375°F). Arrange the zucchini and spring onion over the base of the tart shell so they're evenly distributed. Crumble the feta over the top.

Give the custard a stir to evenly disperse the ingredients, then transfer it to a jug to make filling the quiche easier. Slide out your oven shelf, place the tin on the shelf, then pour the custard into the shell, being very careful not to overfill it. Or fill it on the bench and carefully transfer to the oven. Scatter the sunflower seeds over the top.

Bake for 10 minutes, then reduce the oven to 160°C (320°F). Bake for a further 30–35 minutes, turning the tin halfway through, until the centre of the quiche feels firm but still has a slight wobble. It should be firm rather than runny, but only just cooked. Transfer to a wire rack and cool in the tin for at least 30 minutes to let the custard set. Serve warm or at room temperature. Keeps in the fridge for 3–4 days.

½ quantity Wholemeal flaky shortcrust pastry (page 36)
350 g (12½ oz/2–3) zucchini (courgettes), cut into 1 cm (½ in) thick rounds (see Note)
6 spring onions (scallions), trimmed and cut into 4 cm (1½ in) lengths
granulated sugar or baking weights, for blind baking
250 g (9 oz/5 medium) eggs
240 g (8½ oz) milk kefir
240 g (8½ oz) cream
1 tablespoon finely chopped rosemary
grated zest of 1 lemon
1½ teaspoons fine salt
½ teaspoon freshly ground black pepper
80 g (2¾ oz) feta
20 g (¾ oz) sunflower seeds

Note: If you have zucchini flowers, use four or five on top of the quiche as a beautiful garnish. Add them after you have scattered the sunflower seeds over the top.

ZUCCHINI, GOAT'S CHEESE AND ROSEMARY LOAF
MAKES 8-10 SLICES

This is perfect for a transportable meal or snack – a healthy, sugar-free and sustaining bake that will keep you going until dinnertime. You can use any flour instead of rye for this loaf – spelt and wholemeal also work well with the zucchini.

---

4 medium zucchini (courgettes)
20 g (¾ oz/1 tablespoon) olive oil
1 medium onion, finely diced
½ teaspoon caraway seeds
1 tablespoon chopped rosemary
225 g (8 oz) plain (all-purpose) flour
100 g (3½ oz) rye flour or wholegrain rye flour
18 g (⅔ oz/3 teaspoons) baking powder
¼ teaspoon fine salt
250 g (9 oz/5 medium) eggs, at room temperature
60 g (2 oz) cheddar, coarsely grated
150 g (5½ oz) soft goat's cheese
50 g (1¾ oz) walnuts

Preheat the oven to 180°C (360°F). Grease and line a 10 × 25 cm (4 × 10 in), 8 cm (3¼ in) deep loaf tin, leaving the paper overhanging the long sides by 2–3 cm (¾–1¼ in).

Using a mandoline or sharp knife, cut three long slices of zucchini, about 2 mm (⅟₁₆ in) thick. Save these to garnish the top of your loaf. Coarsely grate the remaining zucchini over a colander. Squeeze the grated zucchini to release any liquid – you should have about 350 g (12½ oz) zucchini. It doesn't matter if you have a little bit more or less, you just want it to be as dry as possible or your loaf will be soggy.

Heat the olive oil in a medium frying pan over a medium heat. Add the onion and cook with the lid on, stirring occasionally, for 10–12 minutes until translucent. Add the caraway seeds and rosemary and cook, stirring, for a few minutes until fragrant and there is a bit of colour on the onion. Set aside to cool.

Put the flours, baking powder and salt in a medium bowl and whisk to combine, removing any lumps. Gently whisk the eggs in a large bowl. Add the cheddar, crumble in the goat's cheese and stir to combine. Add the dry ingredients to the egg mixture and stir until combined, then add the grated zucchini. Use your hands or a spoon to mix until just combined.

Spoon the mixture into the prepared tin and smooth the surface. Lay the reserved sliced zucchini on top, then scatter over the walnuts. Bake on the top oven shelf for 50–60 minutes, turning the tin halfway through, until the loaf is light golden on top and a skewer inserted into the middle comes out clean. If it is not ready and getting too dark on top, reduce the oven to 160°C (320°F) and cover the top of the loaf with aluminium foil to protect it from burning.

Leave in the tin for 10 minutes, then turn out on a wire rack to cool completely. The loaf keeps for 3–4 days in an airtight container, or it can be sliced and frozen, then toasted or warmed in the oven for 6 minutes at 160°C (320°F).

SWEET CORN AND SOUR CREAM LOAF
MAKES 8-10 SLICES

This makes an excellent snack or brunch dish served with avocado and sour cream. It's based on all the things that make a great sweet corn fritter, but in a loaf form. If you like, substitute the buttermilk for milk kefir or a 50:50 mix of milk and plain yoghurt.

———

3 corn cobs
20 g (¾ oz) unsalted butter, plus 110 g (4 oz) unsalted butter, melted
½ teaspoon crushed coriander seeds
190 g (6½ oz) plain (all-purpose) flour
150 g (5½ oz) polenta
18 g (⅔ oz/3 teaspoons) baking powder
12 g (½ oz/2 teaspoons) fine salt
250 g (9 oz) buttermilk
120 g (4½ oz) sour cream
40 g (1½ oz) honey
180 g (6½ oz/approx. 4 medium or 3 large) eggs, at room temperature
grated zest and juice of 1 lime
2 spring onions (scallions), trimmed and thinly sliced
18 g (⅔ oz) coriander (cilantro) leaves, chopped
1 red chilli, seeded and finely chopped
30 g (1 oz) parmesan, coarsely grated

Preheat the oven to 180°C (360°F). Grease and line a 10 × 25 cm (4 × 10 in), 8 cm (3¼ in) deep loaf tin, leaving the paper overhanging the long sides by 2–3 cm (¾–1¼ in).

Slice the kernels off the corn cobs. Melt the 20 g (¾ oz) butter in a large frying pan over a medium heat. Pan-fry two-thirds of the corn kernels for 5 minutes, or until they soften and have a little colour. Add the crushed coriander seeds and fry for a further 1–2 minutes until fragrant, then set aside to cool.

Put the flour, polenta, baking powder and salt in a large bowl and whisk to combine, removing any lumps. In a separate bowl, whisk together the melted butter, buttermilk, sour cream, honey, eggs, lime zest and juice until well combined. Pour the buttermilk mixture into the dry ingredients and whisk until well combined with no lumps. Add the fried corn, spring onion, chopped coriander and chilli and mix until just combined.

Pour the mixture into the prepared tin. Combine the parmesan and remaining corn kernels in a small bowl and scatter evenly over the top of the loaf. Bake on the top oven shelf for 45 minutes, then reduce the oven to 160°C (320°F) and turn the tin. Bake for a further 8–10 minutes until golden on top and a skewer inserted into the middle comes out clean. When you touch the loaf, it should feel springy to touch. If it is not ready and getting too dark on top, turn your oven down a little sooner and cover the top of the loaf with aluminium foil to protect it from burning.

Leave in the tin for 10 minutes, then turn out on a wire rack. Serve while still warm. The loaf keeps for 3–4 days in an airtight container, or it can be sliced and frozen, then toasted or warmed in the oven for 6 minutes at 160°C (320°F).

SAUSAGES IN SCRAPS

MAKES 4

EASY TO ADAPT
MAKE IT GLUTEN-FREE
Use gluten-free flaky pastry

This recipe came about as a way of using up scraps of dough. I think it works especially well with puff pastry, but flaky pastry will do the job, too.

We're lucky to get excellent cheese kransky from our local butcher, but any sausage will work. I also like it with cumberland or hot dog sausages. The pastry provides visual novelty and something to hold your sausage with. They're perfect for a school lunch box, weeknight dinners and picnics.

——

Take your pastry scraps and push them all together into a block 2–3 cm (¾–1¼ in) high. Cover and rest in the fridge for 30 minutes.

Preheat the oven to 190°C (375°F). Line a baking tray with baking paper. Put the pastry block on a lightly floured kitchen bench and roll it out into a long sheet 3 mm (⅛ in) thick. Cut the pastry lengthways into strips about 2 cm (¾ in) wide (the exact length is not so important).

Starting from one end of a sausage, coil the pastry strip around it, overlapping each coil with a little of the next so there are no gaps. If your pastry strip ends before you get to the end of the sausage, just take another strip, pinch them together and carry on until the whole sausage is wrapped, with just the ends exposed. Pinch to seal the pastry at the end. Repeat with the remaining sausages and pastry strips.

Lay the wrapped sausages on the lined tray, with the seals underneath, and lightly brush the pastry with egg wash. Bake for about 30 minutes, turning the tray halfway through, until the pastry is golden and flaky. Leave to rest on the tray for 10 minutes. Serve with veggies and Tomato ketchup (page 194).

approx. 250 g (9 oz) pastry
  scraps
4 sausages, about 16 cm (6¼ in)
  in length
Egg wash (page 15)

PORK PIES
MAKES 8

I could not write a savoury baking book without including one of my favourite foods – the humble pork pie. I have been eating these for longer than I can remember, but I admit I had actually never made one until I started working on this book. I was chatting with my friend Mik about them when I realised I had to make one. So, here is my version: hot water pastry and pork mince with herbs and spices.

Pork pies are the perfect picnic food, always served cold. They go nicely with brown sauce, pickles and real ale. Cheers Mik.

The pastry, jelly and mince can be made in advance to take the time pressure off, and then you can have fun assembling them. It's a lot easier than you may think and the pastry is very forgiving. Ask your butcher to mince the pork for you; it will save a lot of time.

JELLY STOCK
2 pig's trotters
1 medium carrot, roughly chopped
1 medium onion, roughly chopped
1 medium leek, roughly chopped
1 celery stalk, roughly chopped
2 fresh bay leaves
1 tablespoon black peppercorns
½ teaspoon salt
1 litre (34 fl oz) water

FILLING
1 kg (2 lb 3 oz) pork shoulder, coarsely minced (ground) or finely chopped
200 g (7 oz) pork belly, skin off, coarsely minced (ground) or finely chopped
200 g (7 oz) smoky bacon, finely chopped
2 tablespoons chopped sage
3 teaspoons fine salt
2 teaspoons freshly ground black pepper
½ teaspoon ground mace
¼ teaspoon cayenne pepper

TO ASSEMBLE
1 quantity Hot water pastry, at room temperature (page 42)
Egg wash (page 15)

To make the jelly stock, put all the ingredients in a medium saucepan and bring to the boil over a medium–high heat, skimming off any impurities. Reduce the heat to low and simmer for 2 hours, then strain the stock into a clean saucepan. Return to a medium heat and reduce by one-third; you will need around 400 g (14 oz) of stock. It keeps in the fridge for up to 5 days or in the freezer for 1 month.

To make the filling, put all the ingredients in a medium bowl and mix well. I like to check the seasoning by frying off a little bit of the mix and tasting it. Adjust to your taste, then refrigerate until you're ready to assemble the pies.

To assemble, divide the pork filling into eight 180 g (6½ oz) balls, then flatten them slightly into rounds 7 cm (2¾ in) in diameter and 5 cm (2 in) high.

Put the pastry on a lightly floured kitchen bench and divide it into eight 100 g (3½ oz) pieces for the bases and eight 50 g (1¾ oz) balls for the lids. Roll the bases into circles 15 cm (6 in) in diameter and 4–5 mm (⅛–¼ in) thick. Roll the lids into circles 10 cm (4 in) in diameter and 4–5 mm (⅛–¼ in) thick. Use a piping nozzle or cutter to make a small hole in the centre of the lids for the jelly to go into at the end.

Lay the bases over the pie filling, then use your hands to shape the pastry around the filling so the top and sides are covered. Flip each one over and gently stretch the edge of the pastry up so it sits slightly higher than the filling.

RECIPE CONTINUES

Lightly brush the lids with egg wash and place one over the top of each pie, egg-washed side down, onto the collar of the pastry base. Use your fingers to press together the base and lid of the pastry. The lid will resemble an upside-down hat at this point. Pinch or crimp around the edges towards the middle of the pie (see image opposite) to fully seal and decorate your pies. Refrigerate for at least 1 hour.

To bake the pies, preheat the oven to 160°C (320°F). Line two baking trays with baking paper. Put the pies on the lined trays and generously brush all over with egg wash. Bake for 1 hour, then turn and swap the trays so the top tray finishes baking on the bottom shelf, and vice versa. Bake for a further 30 minutes, or until the pastry is golden. Check the internal temperature of the pork – it should be 85°C (185°F). Transfer to a wire rack to cool completely.

Heat the jelly slightly until it is liquid but not hot. Use a kitchen syringe or small funnel to pour around 50 g (1¾ oz) of jelly into the hole of each cold pie (or until full), then set aside to cool and set. The pork pies will keep for several days in the fridge.

ONION AND GRUYÈRE GOUGÈRES
MAKES 18

Gougères are moreish bites of cheesy choux pastry. Originally from Burgundy, they are traditionally served with an aperitif but are good at any time.

This is a hugely satisfying bake. I love playing with different flavour combinations: cheese and wholegrain mustard, mushroom and onion or chilli and herbs are all great. The choux bakes up into feathery light balls and even if they don't all end up looking perfect, they'll still be delicious. Just make sure you guard them until needed – they tend to disappear pretty quickly.

---

1 quantity Choux pastry (page 44)
50 g (1¾ oz) Caramelised onions (page 209)
40 g (1½ oz) gruyère, finely grated, plus extra for sprinkling
1 teaspoon chopped thyme
¼ teaspoon freshly ground black pepper
Egg wash (page 15)

Preheat the oven to 190°C (375°F). Line two baking trays with baking paper.

Put the choux pastry in a bowl and add the caramelised onion, cheese, thyme and pepper. Mix with a wooden spoon until just combined. Transfer the choux to a piping bag fitted with a 12 mm (½ in) nozzle. Pipe 18 mounds on the lined trays, about 3 cm (1¼ in) high and 3.5 cm (1½ in) in diameter at the base, spacing them 5 cm (2 in) apart. If you don't have a piping bag, use two spoons to portion the choux. With damp fingers, shape each piece into a smooth sphere. Lightly brush the surface with egg wash and sprinkle with a little extra cheese.

Bake for 10 minutes, then reduce the oven to 180°C (360°F) and bake for a further 10 minutes. Turn and swap the trays, then bake for another 5 minutes, or until the gougères are deep golden and look like light, airy puffballs. To help dry them out more and develop a lovely crust, turn off the oven and leave them in the oven with the door ajar for 10 minutes, or until cooled.

They are amazing straight from the oven but also eat well cold. Store for a few days in an airtight container at room temperature, then reheat in the oven for 5 minutes at 180°C (360°F).

OLIVE, ROSEMARY AND SEA SALT FOCACCIA
MAKES 1 LOAF

This crowd-pleaser is a great introduction to bread making. It's baked in a tray so no technical shaping skills are required. Kids love to get their hands into the dough and have fun arranging the toppings. Olive and rosemary is a classic combination, but I also love it with onions, anchovy, tomato or roasted garlic and a drizzle of balsamic vinegar.

The dough can be made by hand or in an electric stand mixer, although the dough will be stronger if made in a mixer. Instructions for both methods are included. I prefer to use a deep-sided tray for baking this, so the dough and oil are contained. This also helps the edges crisp up better during the bake and it won't dry out after baking.

The key to success here is a healthy sourdough starter fed at least three times before using it. I feed it the night before and then make the dough first thing in the morning. I recommend the following feed schedule:

Day 1   Take 20 g (¾ oz/1 tablespoon) Sourdough starter (page 18) and feed it with 20 g (¾ oz/1 tablespoon) water plus 15 g (½ oz/1 tablespoon) bakers (strong) flour.

Day 2   Feed your starter in the morning with 20 g (¾ oz/1 tablespoon) water and 15 g (½ oz/1 tablespoon) bakers (strong) flour. In the evening, feed it with 40 g (1½ oz/2 tablespoons) water plus 30 g (1 oz/2 tablespoons) bakers (strong) flour. This will give you enough starter for the recipe plus a little left over for continuation.

Day 3   Start the focaccia in the morning following the method below, when the starter is ripe and bubbly from its previous feed.

――――

DOUGH
600 g (1 lb 5 oz) bakers (strong) flour
460 g (1 lb) water
120 g (4½ oz) Sourdough starter (see Day 1–3, above)
12 g (¼ oz/2 teaspoons) fine salt
15 g (½ oz/3 teaspoons) olive oil, plus extra for drizzling

TOPPING
3–4 rosemary sprigs, leaves picked
pinch of flaky sea salt
80 g (2¾ oz) pitted green and black olives

To make the dough by hand, combine the flour, 410 g (14½ oz) of the water, starter and salt in a medium bowl. Mix with your hands until you have a cohesive mass, then scrape down the bowl with your hands. Stretch and fold the dough for about 5 minutes to build up the dough structure. Use the windowpane test to check the dough. Take a small piece of dough and stretch it between your hands – it should stretch enough to be almost transparent without breaking. Once it is getting stronger and if it is not too sticky, mix in the remaining 50 g (1¾ oz/2½ tablespoons) water followed by the olive oil. Continue mixing for a further 5–6 minutes. The dough will be quite wet and sticky, but don't worry; the pan will hold it together.

RECIPE CONTINUES

To make the dough in a mixer, combine the flour, 410 g (14½ oz) of the water, starter and salt in the bowl. Mix with the dough hook on medium speed for 5 minutes, or until it all comes together. Scrape down the side of the bowl, then add the remaining 50 g (1¾ oz/2½ tablespoons) water and the olive oil. Continue to mix on medium speed for 5 minutes, or until the dough is smooth and quite elastic. Check the dough with the windowpane test (see page 143).

Cover the dough in the bowl with a damp tea towel (dish towel) and rest for 30 minutes at room temperature.

The dough is now ready to be folded. Give the dough a set of folds every 30 minutes for the first 2 hours. To fold, wet your hands, then use one hand to hold the bowl and the other to fold. Grab a piece of dough on the side of the bowl, then pull and stretch it up and over the middle to the other side of the bowl. Repeat this six to eight times, moving around the edge of the bowl. Cover and rest the dough between each set of folds. It should become very strong and stretchy over time.

After the last set of folds, cover and rest the dough in a warm place for 2 hours. Ideally the temperature should be around 24–26°C (75–79°F). If the room is too cold, put the dough in your (cold) oven with the light on, with a tray of hot water at the bottom to create warmth and humidity. When it's ready, you should see pockets of air on the surface of the dough and it should wobble if you shake the tray. Another test is to gently poke the dough. If your fingertip leaves a dent, it's ready, but if the dough springs back quickly, cover again and give it more time.

If you want to bake your focaccia the next day, cover it with a damp tea towel and refrigerate. When you are ready to bake, let it come up to room temperature and finish proving as below.

Line a 22.5 × 33 cm (9 × 13 in) deep-sided baking tray with baking paper or grease with a generous amount of olive oil. Wet your hands and put the dough in the middle of the tray, then use your fingertips to gently stretch the dough into the corners so it is fairly even in depth. Cover and leave in a warm place to prove. The proving time is variable and depends on the temperature of the room: if it's cool, let it prove longer; if it's warm, you will be able to bake sooner. As a guide, it should take 1½–2 hours if the temperature is around 24–26°C (75–79°F). The dough is ready when it has risen by half and is nice and bubbly – it should wobble slightly if you shake the tray. Use the fingerprint method, as above, to check if the dough is ready.

Preheat the oven to 230°C (450°F) about 20 minutes before you are ready to bake. Put one shelf at the top of the oven for the focaccia and one below with a small shallow tray on it for the water.

Drizzle a little olive oil over the top of the focaccia. Oil your fingertips and gently push them into the dough until you can feel the bottom of the tray, then repeat, leaving space between each press. Scatter over the rosemary and salt, then press the olives gently into the dough, leaving them exposed on top.

Put the focaccia on the top shelf and pour 100 g (3½ oz) boiling water into the tray on the bottom. This will create steam, which will help the dough rise during the initial part of the bake. Bake for 25–28 minutes until golden on top, turning the tray and removing the steam tray halfway through the bake.

Leave to cool in the tray for a couple of minutes, then tip it out onto a wire rack. This focaccia is wonderful to eat while still hot from the oven, but will keep well, wrapped in cloth or a paper bag, for a few days – that's if you manage to resist eating it all on day one.

PUFF

FENNEL
BULBS

LATER

18 ELEGANT EVENING AFFAIRS
PAGES 148–185

LATER

What to eat for dinner? More pies certainly, but shifting perhaps into more sophisticated territory, with some bolder flavours and often underutilised ingredients.

In Australia, kangaroo and wallaby represent a more sustainable choice if you choose to eat meat. The meat comes from wild animals, a by-product of population control programmes. The animals roam freely eating their natural diet, and the meat is free of hormones, rich in iron and protein. Their lean, gamey meat works well with the bold flavours in the kangaroo, preserved lemon and prune pie or the wallaby and harissa sausage roll.

The beetroot and shallot tarte tatin and the pumpkin galette are both weeknight staples at our place. In winter, I can't go past a warming curry pie, either butter chicken or an Indian-style vegetable version, helped down by a nice ale or beer.

Step it up a notch with the root wellington or mushroom pithivier. These showstoppers celebrate vegetables and classic techniques that I learned while working in London restaurants. They are a little more involved but well worth the effort. I like to break down the steps by preparing some elements in advance so I can relax before dinner.

The recipes in this chapter are a bit of a melting pot and represent years of cooking and baking, both at home and professionally. I hope you enjoy exploring the different flavours and textures here.

GRAN'S TRADITIONAL CORNISH PASTY TARTS
MAKES 2; SERVES 4–6 EACH

MAKE IT GLUTEN-FREE
Use gluten-free flaky pastry

Gran's pasty tart was something I looked forward to every Friday evening when I was young. It's basically a traditional Cornish pasty but in tart form. Simply take an old enamel deep pie dish, line it with lard pastry, fill and top your tart and then bake it. Gran always called it a pasty tart, but I gather from asking around other Cornish folk that most call it a pasty pie. It's just swede, potato, onion and really good skirt steak. 'Ansum!

Put the pastry on a lightly floured kitchen bench and divide it into two equal pieces. Roll out into two rectangles roughly measuring 30 × 60 cm (12 × 23½ in). Roll one 2 mm (1/16 in) thick and the other 3 mm (1/8 in) thick, then cut two 30 cm (12 in) discs from each. The thinner pastry is for the tart bases and the thicker one is for the tops. Put the pastry discs on a tray, layering a piece of baking paper between each one. Add the two pastry tops to the tray first, then the two bases last. Put in the fridge to rest for 20 minutes.

Grease two 26 cm (10¼ in) round, 5 cm (2 in) deep pie dishes. Gently lay the pastry bases over the dishes, then use your thumb to firmly press the pastry into the corners. Rest again in the fridge while you prepare the filling.

Peel and chop the onions, swedes and potatoes into randomly shaped pieces, roughly 1.5–2 cm (½–¾ in) in size. Cut the beef into 1 cm (½ in) dice.

Combine the vegetables and beef in a large bowl. Add the salt and white pepper and mix well. Divide the mixture between the two pie dishes – about 850 g (1 lb 14 oz) each. Lightly brush the rims with egg wash, then lay the pastry tops over the filling so the edges meet. Press the edges together to seal, pushing out any air as you do this. Crimp or pinch around the edge with your thumb and forefinger, using both hands. Brush all over the top with egg wash, then use a knife to poke a couple of holes in the top to allow the steam to vent while baking.

Return the pasty tarts to the fridge to rest while you preheat the oven to 190°C (375°F). If you only want to bake one tart, the other will keep in the fridge for 2–3 days, or freeze it for up to 3 months.

Bake for 10 minutes, then reduce the oven to 160°C (320°F). Bake for a further 60–70 minutes, turning the tarts halfway through, until the pastry turns a lovely golden brown. Transfer to a wire rack to rest for at least 10 minutes before eating.

The pictured tart was made using wholemeal lard shortcrust pastry.

1 quantity Lard shortcrust pastry (page 38)
400 g (14 oz) onions
280 g (10 oz) swedes (rutabagas)
280 g (10 oz) potatoes
800 g (1 lb 12 oz) beef skirt or chuck steak
20 g (¾ oz) flaky sea salt
1 teaspoon white pepper
Egg wash (page 15)

FISH PIE
SERVES 6-8

EASY TO ADAPT
MAKE IT GLUTEN-FREE
Use gluten-free flaky pastry, flour and mustard

This is a classic and comforting dish for all seasons, a chance to enjoy the beauty of fish. I grew up near the Newlyn Fish Market in Cornwall, where we had access to all kinds of fish – cod, haddock, mackerel, bass … I like a combination of textures and flavours for this pie, so use a mix of smoked fish, white fish, oily fish, and scallops or prawns. Use whatever you like or vary it based on what's available at the market or fishmonger.

Fish is expensive now and so it should be, so make sure you use it all to stretch the value. Save yourself some work and ask your fishmonger to fillet whole fish and give you the skin and bones (you usually pay for it anyway). As you prepare your ingredients, set aside the prawn shells and vegetable trimmings, then use them to make a quick stock. Put it all in a saucepan and cover with water. Bring to a gentle boil and simmer for 20 minutes, then remove from the heat to cool before straining.

First prepare your seafood. Shell the prawns and cut all the fish into 2–3 cm (¾–1¼ in) pieces, then put it all in the fridge. Use the trimmings to make a quick stock as described above.

Heat the olive oil in a large heavy-based saucepan over a low–medium heat. Add the fennel, shallot, leek and garlic and cook with the lid on, stirring occasionally, for about 10 minutes, or until softened but not browned. Transfer to a large bowl.

Return the pan to a medium heat and melt the butter. Add the flour and whisk to combine. Cook, whisking, for 4–5 minutes until the mixture darkens slightly and resembles sand. Add the fish stock, whisking if necessary to get rid of any lumps, then add the milk and bring to the boil. Reduce the heat to low and simmer for 2–3 minutes until the béchamel thickens. It should be like very thick custard. Set aside to cool.

Add the prawns, fish and béchamel to the fennel mixture. Add the chives, parsley, fennel fronds, lemon zest and juice, mustard, salt and pepper and stir to combine well. Transfer to a 23 cm (9 in) square, 8 cm (3¼ in) deep pie dish, or use a similarly sized oval or round dish. Refrigerate while you prepare your pastry.

Put the pastry on a lightly floured kitchen bench and roll it out into a square roughly measuring 28 × 28 cm (11 × 11 in) and 4 mm (⅛ in) thick. Adjust the shape accordingly for differently sized pie dishes. Lay the pastry between two sheets of baking paper and refrigerate for 30 minutes.

Remove the pastry from the fridge and remove the top sheet of paper. To mark the top with 'fish scales', use a measuring spoon or melon baller to gently score semicircle indentations in a line along the top edge of the pastry, making sure that you don't pierce the pastry.

6 raw prawns (shrimp), shells on
700 g (1 lb 9 oz) white fish fillets, such as snapper, blue eye, ling and flathead
200 g (7 oz) hot-smoked fish fillets, such as rainbow trout, flaked
60 g (2 oz) olive oil
2 small fennel bulbs (approx. 250 g/9 oz), thinly sliced and fronds reserved
4 large shallots (approx. 250 g/ 9 oz), thinly sliced
1 small leek, white part only, thinly sliced
2 garlic cloves, finely chopped
70 g (2½ oz) unsalted butter
70 g (2½ oz) plain (all-purpose) flour
300 g (10½ oz) fish or vegetable stock
300 g (10½ oz) full-cream (whole) milk
20 g (¾ oz) snipped chives
10 g (⅓ oz) chopped parsley
grated zest and juice of 1 lemon
10 g (⅓ oz/2 teaspoons) Wholegrain mustard (page 211)
9 g (⅓ oz/1½ teaspoons) fine salt
½ teaspoon freshly ground black pepper

½ quantity Flaky shortcrust (page 36) or Puff pastry (page 32)
Egg wash (page 15)

Follow this with another line directly underneath, offsetting the scales above. Continue all the way down the pastry sheet. Lightly brush the pastry with egg wash, cover with baking paper and return it to the fridge to rest for another 30 minutes.

Slide the pastry off the baking paper and on to the top of the pie dish, with the edges overhanging the side of the dish. Lightly brush the top of the pastry with egg wash again and use a knife to make a couple of steam holes in the top. Return to the fridge for 30 minutes.

To bake the pie, preheat the oven to 180°C (360°F). If your pie dish is very full, it's a good idea to put a tray on the bottom shelf of the oven to catch any bubbling sauce during baking – it's much easier to clean this off a tray than off your oven floor. Bake for 40–45 minutes, turning the dish halfway through, until the pastry is flaky and golden.

Rest for 10 minutes before serving with green beans and peas, or a bitter leafy salad. Enjoy with a nice glass of wine!

The pictured pie was made using wholemeal flaky shortcrust pastry.

BEETROOT AND SHALLOT TARTE TATIN

SERVES 4

EASY TO ADAPT
MAKE IT GLUTEN-FREE
Use gluten-free flaky pastry
MAKE IT VEGAN
Use vegan flaky pastry and plant-based milk for brushing

This is a slightly fancy way to serve simple roasted root vegetables, and once you have the vegetables roasted and the pastry made, it's a quick dish to assemble. I recommend prepping everything the day before.

Back in my restaurant days, we used to do a little tarte tatin of banana shallots. I love the idea of something that's traditionally sweet as a savoury dish. It's very simple to make, so satisfying to eat and can look spectacular on the dining table as a showpiece.

Line your tatin pan with a circle of baking paper the same diameter as the base; this makes it easier to turn the tarte out and keep the form of the vegetables. I've used puff here but flaky shortcrust pastry will also work well. I have made this with all sorts of root veg, such as carrots, celeriac and fennel, so you have plenty of options and can experiment to your taste.

———

Put the pastry on a lightly floured kitchen bench and roll it out into a disc 4 mm (⅛ in) thick, then cut a circle 1 cm (½ in) wider than your pan. I use a 25 cm (10 in) round tarte tatin pan. Lay the pastry between two sheets of baking paper and refrigerate until you're ready to assemble.

Preheat the oven to 180°C (360°F). Loosely wrap the peeled garlic cloves in aluminium foil. Put the shallots in a roasting tin, drizzle with 20 g (¾ oz/1 tablespoon) of the olive oil and toss to coat, then sprinkle with the nigella and celery seeds. Add the foil bag with the garlic to the tin and roast for 20 minutes, or until the shallots have a bit of colour and are softened slightly. Set aside to cool.

Increase the oven to 190°C (375°F). Peel the beetroot and cut the larger ones into halves or quarters and leave the baby ones whole. Put in a separate roasting tin, drizzle with the remaining 60 g (2 oz) olive oil and cover the tin with foil. Roast for 30–40 minutes until tender. Set aside to cool.

To assemble the tarte, cut a disc of baking paper the same size as the base of your tatin pan and line the pan.

Combine the sugar, pomegranate molasses, vinegar and water in a small saucepan over a medium heat. Cook, stirring, until the sugar dissolves, then bring to the boil for a few minutes until the mixture becomes quite syrupy – just before it starts to caramelise. Remove the pan from the heat when you see lots of medium-sized bubbles on top.

½ quantity Puff pastry (page 32)
6 garlic cloves, whole and peeled
6 medium shallots, peeled with roots left intact
80 g (2¾ oz) olive oil
1 tablespoon nigella seeds
1 teaspoon celery seeds
700 g (1 lb 9 oz) small beetroot
60 g (2 oz) soft brown sugar
60 g (2 oz) pomegranate molasses (see Note)
30 g (1 oz/1½ tablespoons) balsamic vinegar
30 g (1 oz/1½ tablespoons) water
3–4 thyme sprigs, plus 1 teaspoon chopped thyme
1 teaspoon chopped rosemary
Egg wash (page 15)
flaky sea salt
freshly ground black pepper

Note: If you do not have access to pomegranate molasses, substitute with balsamic vinegar.

Pour the caramel into the prepared pan and spread it evenly over the base. Set aside to cool for a few minutes. Lay the thyme sprigs over the caramel in the pan and arrange the beetroot, cut side up, on top. Squeeze the shallots and garlic in between the beetroot so that everything is snug, then sprinkle over the chopped herbs. Lay the pastry sheet over the top, tucking the edges in between the vegetables and the side of the pan. Lightly brush the top of the pastry with egg wash and use a knife to make a couple of steam holes in the top. Refrigerate for 30 minutes to set the pastry, or until ready to bake.

Preheat the oven to 190°C (375°F). Bake the tarte tatin for 25 minutes, then reduce the oven to 180°C (360°F) and turn the pan. Bake for a further 15 minutes, or until the pastry is deep golden and puffed and flaky on top.

Rest for 10 minutes before inverting it onto your serving dish and removing the paper disc. Be careful not to burn yourself on the caramel! Season to taste with salt and pepper. Serve with a green salad and some goat's curd or cheese.

Pictured on page 158.

MUSHROOM, RYE AND PRESERVED LEMON PITHIVIERS
SERVES 4

MAKE IT GLUTEN-FREE
Use gluten-free flaky pastry

The idea for this recipe came about after I ate the tastiest and most wholesome sausage roll at Staple Bread in Sydney. The combination of rye puff pastry and mushrooms works so well, and the addition of preserved lemon and parmesan provides salt and umami. This makes for a wonderfully flavoursome and good-looking dinner, and it's great for a dinner party as everything is prepared the day before – just put it in the oven on the night.

You can use any mushrooms depending on availability – portobello, chestnut, field mushrooms or shiitakes. They're all good. Mushrooms can vary in the amount of moisture they have. If they're holding a lot of water after cooking, drain well in a colander, pat dry with paper towel or squeeze out any excess water with your hands after they have cooled down. If you don't have preserved lemon, use the grated zest of one lemon to add that citrus flavour.

Put the pastry on a lightly floured kitchen bench and roll it out into a rectangle measuring 30 × 65 cm (12 × 25½ in) and 3 mm (⅛ in) thick. Working along the length of the pastry, cut out four small discs 13 cm (5 in) in diameter for the base, and four larger discs 15 cm (6 in) in diameter for the tops. Lay the pastry between two sheets of baking paper and refrigerate for 20 minutes, or until you are ready to assemble the pithiviers.

Melt 20 g (¾ oz) of the butter with 20 g (¾ oz/1 tablespoon) of the olive oil in a medium frying pan over a medium heat. Add the onion, garlic and herbs and cook with the lid on, stirring occasionally, for about 10 minutes, or until soft and translucent.

Meanwhile, melt the remaining 20 g (¾ oz) butter and 20 g (¾ oz/ 1 tablespoon) olive oil in a large frying pan over a medium heat. Fry the mushrooms for 4–5 minutes until they start to turn golden. You may need to do this in batches depending on the size of your pan. Add a squeeze of lemon juice as you finish cooking each batch, then transfer the mushrooms to a colander set over a bowl to drain. Set aside to cool.

Combine the mushrooms, onion mixture, parmesan, preserved lemon, salt and pepper in a large bowl. Taste and check for seasoning and adjust to your taste. Set aside for 1 hour, or overnight, to cool and allow the flavours to marry.

To assemble, divide the mushroom mixture into four equal portions, about 150 g (5½ oz) each. Cup your hands over the mushroom mixture to form a tight ball, repeating for each portion. Put them on a tray and chill in the fridge while you get your pastry ready.

1 quantity Rye puff pastry (page 32)
40 g (1½ oz) unsalted butter
40 g (1½ oz/2 tablespoons) olive oil
2 medium onions, roughly chopped
2 garlic cloves, finely chopped
1 tablespoon finely chopped thyme
1 tablespoon finely chopped rosemary
450 g (1 lb) mixed mushrooms, chopped into 2 cm (¾ in) pieces
juice of ½ lemon
100 g (3½ oz) parmesan, coarsely grated
20 g (¾ oz) Preserved lemon rind, finely chopped (page 192)
½ teaspoon fine salt
¼ teaspoon freshly ground black pepper
Egg wash (page 15)

Line a baking tray with baking paper. Lay the larger pastry discs on a floured bench and mark the centre of each with a tiny vent hole. Using a pastry cutter or small plate as a template, very lightly score curved lines in the disc, starting from the centre to the edge of the pastry, moving the template around until you have filled the disc. You can do a few curved lines or a lot – get creative!

Lay the smaller pastry discs on the bench and place one portion of mushroom filling in the middle of each. You might feel like there's too much filling, but it's worth piling it up now as it will reduce during baking. Lightly brush around the pastry edges with egg wash, then lay the large discs over the filling. Carefully push the pastry lid down and around the mushrooms, cupping your hands around the filling to seal and straighten it, edging out any air as you go. The edge of the top disc should sit flush with the edge of the bottom disc; carefully ease the top layer out with your fingers if needed. Pinch the edges together with your finger and thumb to seal and crimp the edges. You can also use a fluted pastry cutter or fork to seal and decorate the edges.

Transfer the pithiviers to the lined tray. Lightly brush the tops with egg wash and refrigerate for 1 hour, or overnight, to set the butter back into the pastry and let the egg wash set.

When you're ready to bake, preheat the oven to 190°C (375°F). Bake for 15 minutes, then reduce the oven to 180°C (360°F) and turn the tray. Bake for a further 20 minutes, or until golden. Transfer to a wire rack to cool for 10 minutes before serving.

Pictured on page 159.

RABBIT, BACON AND WHITE BEAN PIE
SERVES 6-8

I love sharing this simple supper with friends on a cold evening. The braise is toothsome and flavourful, and I love the texture the white beans add. Top with flaky pastry and then all it needs is a bitter leaf salad and a bottle of light red to make a meal.

Rabbits are an introduced pest in Australia. They cause a lot of erosion and habitat destruction, so for me they land in the category of sustainable meat choices. The meat is tasty and lean and is not difficult to prepare – you can braise it on the bone until it falls away, or ask your butcher to debone it and keep the bones to make a stock. If you do not have access to rabbit, you can substitute with chicken or pheasant.

Start this recipe the day before to give the beans time to soak overnight, and be sure to keep the fat on the bacon for maximum flavour.

Heat a large heavy-based saucepan or cast-iron casserole dish over a medium–high heat and melt the butter. Brown the rabbit pieces in batches and set aside.

Add the bacon to the pan and fry for 5 minutes, or until the fat has released and the bacon is starting to brown. Add the onion and leek, then reduce the heat to medium and cook, stirring occasionally, for 8–10 minutes until starting to soften. Add the carrot, garlic, rosemary and thyme and cook for a further 5 minutes or so, until fragrant and well mixed.

Return the rabbit to the pan, add the stock and beans and stir to combine well. Bring to the boil, then reduce the heat to low, cover partially with the lid and simmer for 1½ hours.

Remove the rabbit pieces and increase the heat to reduce the sauce by half. Add the cavolo nero and mix it through the sauce.

When the rabbit is cool enough to handle, pick the meat off the bones, being very careful not to miss any bones. (You can keep the bones to roast and make a stock for your next pie.) Dice any larger pieces of meat, then mix it all back through the sauce. Season to taste with salt and pepper. Refrigerate for a few hours or overnight before assembling and baking your pie(s) (see page 22).

30 g (1 oz) unsalted butter
1 rabbit (approx. 1.5 kg/3 lb 5 oz), jointed
6 rashers thick-cut streaky bacon (150 g/5½ oz), sliced
1 large onion, roughly chopped
1 medium leek, white part only, sliced
2 large carrots, roughly chopped
3 garlic cloves, finely chopped
3 rosemary sprigs, leaves picked and chopped
3 thyme sprigs, leaves picked
1 litre (34 fl oz) rabbit, chicken or vegetable stock
100 g (3½ oz) dried white beans, soaked overnight in plenty of water, drained
½ bunch cavolo nero, leaves picked and chopped (85 g/ 3 oz picked weight)
fine salt
freshly ground black pepper
pastry of choice (see Pie basics, page 22)

LAMB SHOULDER, ROSEMARY AND BARLEY PIE
SERVES 6

I've been making variations of this lamb pie for years. It has all the wonderful classic pairings for lamb – rosemary, red wine, tomato, garlic and barley. These were my mum's favourite ingredients. When I was growing up in Cornwall, she often used to make a lamb roast with rosemary and lots of garlic. So I turned it into an easy, delicious pie.

The flour helps thicken the braise and gives it more body, but you can leave it out if you want to make it gluten-free, or use cornflour instead. If you don't have red wine, use stock or water.

——

800 g (1 lb 12 oz) boneless lamb shoulder, cut into 2 cm (¾ in) dice
50 g (1¾ oz) plain (all-purpose) flour
40–60 g (1½–2 oz) olive oil
2 medium onions, cut into 2–3 cm (¾–1¼ in) dice
2 medium carrots, cut into 2 cm (¾ in) pieces
1 medium leek, white part only, thickly sliced
4 garlic cloves, sliced
50 g (2 oz) tomato paste (concentrated purée)
1 × 400 g (14 oz) tin chopped tomatoes or 400 g (14 oz) fresh tomatoes (see Note)
2 fresh bay leaves
1 tablespoon chopped rosemary
600 g (1 lb 5 oz) red wine, chicken stock or water
100 g (3½ oz) pearl barley
20 g (¾ oz/1 tablespoon) balsamic vinegar
2 teaspoons fine salt
½ teaspoon freshly ground black pepper
pastry of choice (see Pie basics, page 22)

Note: If using fresh tomatoes, blanch them in hot water for 15–20 seconds, then plunge into iced water. Drain, remove the skins, then roughly chop.

Put the lamb and flour in a large bowl and toss to coat.

Heat a large heavy-based saucepan or cast-iron casserole dish over a medium–high heat, then add 20 g (¾ oz/1 tablespoon) of the olive oil. Brown the lamb in batches, adding more oil as required. Set aside in a large bowl.

Return the pan to a medium heat and add another 20 g (¾ oz/ 1 tablespoon) olive oil. Cook the onion, carrot, leek and garlic for about 5 minutes, or until lightly browned. Add the tomato paste, tomatoes, bay leaves, rosemary, wine, barley, vinegar, salt and pepper. If you're using tinned tomatoes, rinse out the tin with the wine to get all the goodness of the tomato.

Bring to the boil, then reduce the heat to low and simmer with the lid on for 1½ hours, or until the lamb is slightly tender. The mixture should have a thick sauce-like consistency. Once it's cooled a little, check the seasoning, adding more salt and pepper, to taste. Refrigerate for a few hours or overnight before assembling and baking your pie(s) (see page 22).

ROOT
WELLINGTON
SERVES 4

This dish is a bit of a showstopper. It's a vegetarian version of the classic beef wellington, a celebration of root vegetables wrapped in cabbage and mushrooms and then encased in flaky puff pastry. There are quite a few elements to prepare and I recommend doing most of the prep jobs the day before you plan to eat it. But it is fun to make if you want to be more adventurous and expand your repertoire. There's enough going on here to make every mouthful varied and exciting.

Use your favourite root vegetables or whatever is in season. The vegetables are roasted and cooled prior to assembly to soften them slightly and give them a bit of colour and flavour. Take a moment to think about how long different vegetables take to cook and roast like with like. For example, carrots and potatoes can be cooked together as they take longer to cook than sweeter vegetables such as Jerusalem artichokes, celeriac or parsnip.

The recipe uses black garlic, which is made by slowly cooking garlic over several weeks. The garlic is held at a stable temperature and humidity level, which, over a prolonged period, causes the Maillard reaction to change the colour and structure of the garlic. The result is jet-black garlic cloves similar in texture to soft dried fruit. It tastes slightly caramelised, with a softer flavour than raw garlic. Black garlic is delicious as is, on toast, or used to round out a dish like this. You can substitute roasted garlic – just chuck whole, unpeeled cloves in with the vegetables when you roast them, then peel them before assembling your wellington.

———

1 quantity Puff pastry (page 32)

PREPARE YOUR PASTRY
Line a tray with baking paper. Put the pastry on a lightly floured kitchen bench and roll it out into a rectangle roughly measuring 45 × 30 cm (17¾ × 12 in) and 3 mm (⅛ in) thick. Cut out one rectangle 27 × 30 cm (10¾ × 12 in) and another 18 × 30 cm (7 × 12 in). Put the pastry sheets on the lined tray, cover and refrigerate until you're ready to assemble.

INGREDIENTS CONTINUE   *RECIPE CONTINUES*

ROASTED VEGETABLES

Preheat the oven to 190°C (375°F). Put all the vegetables into roasting tins, combining vegetables with similar cooking times. Drizzle with olive oil and toss to coat, then add a few little knobs of butter to the tins and drizzle the vinegar over the top. Roast until the vegetables are slightly soft and starting to colour. The softer vegetables will need about 30 minutes and the harder ones will need 35–45 minutes. Set aside to cool, then drain on paper towel or a clean tea towel (dish towel) to remove any excess oil or liquid. Toss through the parsley and season to taste with salt and pepper.

MUSHROOM LAYER

While the vegetables are roasting, cut the mushrooms into 1–2 cm (½–¾ in) pieces; quarter small mushrooms like button mushrooms and slice larger ones.

Melt the butter with the olive oil in a large frying pan over a medium heat. Add the onion and garlic and cook with a lid on, stirring occasionally, for about 5 minutes, or until softened. Reduce the heat to low–medium, then add the mushrooms, rosemary, thyme, salt and pepper. Cook with the lid off, stirring occasionally, for 10–15 minutes until the mushrooms have released their liquid and any excess has evaporated. Remove the pan from the heat and allow the mushrooms to cool completely, then coarsely chop with a knife or pulse in a food processor. Put the mushroom mixture in the fridge until you're ready to assemble.

PREPARE THE CABBAGE

Bring a large saucepan of salted water to the boil. Put a bowl of iced water next to the pan. Plunge the cabbage leaves into the boiling water for 90 seconds and then immediately refresh in the iced water. Leave them to cool for a few minutes, then drain and dry well with paper towel or a clean tea towel. Cut off the tough middle stem from each cabbage leaf.

TO ASSEMBLE

Line a baking tray with baking paper. Place a large piece of baking paper on the bench and lightly dust the paper with flour. Lay the 27 × 30 cm (10¾ × 12 in) piece of pastry on top, with one short side parallel with the edge of the bench. Lightly brush a 2 cm (¾ in) border around all four edges with egg wash.

Lay the cabbage leaves over the pastry sheet, avoiding the 2 cm (¾ in) border, overlapping the leaves so there are no gaps. Cut the leaves to fit if necessary. Lightly sprinkle with salt and pepper. Spread the mushroom mixture evenly over the top of the cabbage leaves.

Place the roasted vegetables in a horizontal strip over the bottom third of the pastry sheet. Be mindful that you'll need to roll the vegetables in the pastry, so set some veg aside if you have too much. Scatter the black garlic evenly over the vegetables and season with salt and pepper.

ROASTED VEGETABLES

About 600 g (1 lb 5 oz) peeled, mostly root, vegetables, for example:
- 3 baby carrots
- 4 shallots
- 1 baby fennel, cut in half
- 2 parsnips, cut in half
- 4 Jerusalem artichokes, cut in half
- 1 small swede (rutabaga), cut into 4–5 cm (1½–2 in) pieces
- 1 small celeriac, cut into 4–5 cm (1½–2 in) pieces
- 2 kipfler (fingerling) or chat potatoes, cut in half

olive oil, for drizzling
60 g (2 oz) unsalted butter, chopped
50 g (1¾ oz/2½ tablespoons) balsamic vinegar
1 tablespoon chopped parsley
flaky sea salt
freshly ground black pepper

MUSHROOM LAYER

350 g (12½ oz) mushrooms – use a mix of field, chestnut, button and wild mushrooms
40 g (1½ oz) unsalted butter
20 g (¾ oz/1 tablespoon) olive oil
250 g (9 oz) onions, finely chopped
1 garlic clove, finely chopped
1 teaspoon chopped rosemary
1 teaspoon chopped thyme
1 teaspoon fine salt
¼ teaspoon freshly ground black pepper

TO ASSEMBLE

4 large savoy cabbage leaves, or more smaller ones
Egg wash (page 15)
flaky sea salt
freshly ground black pepper
5 black garlic cloves, cut in quarters

  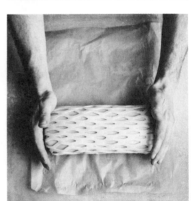

Starting from the side closest to you, use both hands to tightly roll the wellington into a thick cylinder, ending with the seam underneath. You can lift the paper underneath to help you roll it up and over. Use the excess pastry at each end to seal your wellington; lift up the bottom flap and fold the top one over it, tucking the ends underneath. Brush the top and sides with egg wash, then set the roll aside.

Use a lattice cutter or a knife to cut little slits in the remaining pastry sheet in lines parallel with the long edge of the pastry. Vary the size of the slits, so that some are long and some are short. Gently pick up your cut pastry sheet, stretch it out and place it over the top of the roll. Tuck the lattice underneath the wellington on all sides. Lightly brush with egg wash all over. Transfer to the lined tray and refrigerate while you preheat the oven to 180°C (360°F).

When the oven is hot, lightly brush all over the wellington once more with egg wash. Bake for 50–60 minutes, turning the tray halfway, until the pastry is golden, crisp and flaky on the outside. Rest for 10 minutes before serving.

PUMPKIN AND BLUE CHEESE GALETTES

MAKES 2; SERVES 6

EASY TO ADAPT
MAKE IT GLUTEN-FREE
Use gluten-free flaky pastry
MAKE IT VEGAN
Use vegan flaky pastry, use vegan cheese

This is one of my favourite weeknight dinners. If you're in the habit of a weekly meal preparation session, I recommend cooking the pumpkin and making the pastry ahead of time. Once those jobs are done, assembling the two galettes is quick, leaving you time for a cheeky pre-dinner drink while it bakes.

Stilton is my preferred cheese for this galette – it's so creamy and perfectly robust against the sweetness of the pumpkin, but use any cheese you like. You can make many other galettes based on the ideas here: roasted beetroot, goat's cheese and hazelnut; carrots roasted in za'atar with pecorino; sweet potato, harissa, preserved lemon and labne. Let your imagination run wild.

Preheat the oven to 180°C (360°F). Cut the unpeeled pumpkin in half lengthways and scoop out the seeds. Put the pumpkin halves in a roasting tin, cut side up, drizzle with the olive oil and season with salt and pepper. Cover the tin with aluminium foil and bake for 1 hour, or until soft. Set aside to cool completely.

Put the pastry on a lightly floured kitchen bench and divide it into two equal pieces. Roll each piece into a disc 4 mm (⅛ in) thick. Cover and refrigerate for 30 minutes.

Using a large dinner plate as a guide, cut out two rounds from the pastry 30–32 cm (12–12½ in) in diameter. Lightly score a circle 5 cm (2 in) in from the edge of the pastry. Refrigerate again for 30 minutes.

Mash the cooled roasted pumpkin into a rough purée, discarding the skin. Spoon half the purée over each pastry base and spread it out to meet the 5 cm (2 in) margin. Fold the margin of pastry in towards the centre, over the edge of the pumpkin, then crimp the pastry edges together to contain the filling. Lightly brush the exposed pastry border with egg wash.

Return the galettes to the fridge. Preheat the oven to 190°C (375°F). To get the bottom of the pastries nicely browned and cooked through, put two baking trays in the oven to heat up, or use a pizza stone if you have one.

Slide the galettes on the baking paper onto the hot trays. Bake for 15 minutes, then reduce the oven to 180°C (360°F) and turn and swap the trays. Bake for a further 20–25 minutes until the pastry is golden brown. Transfer to a wire rack to cool for a few minutes, then crumble the blue cheese and sprinkle the seeds over the pumpkin. Finish with the herbs and salad leaves and a drizzle of olive oil.

1 large butternut pumpkin (squash) (approx. 1.5 kg/ 3 lb 5 oz)
50 g (1¾ oz/2½ tablespoons) olive oil, plus extra for drizzling
fine salt
freshly ground black pepper
1 quantity Wholemeal flaky shortcrust pastry (page 36)
Egg wash (page 15)
120 g (4½ oz) blue cheese
10 g (⅓ oz) pepitas (pumpkin seeds), lightly toasted
10 g (⅓ oz) sunflower seeds, lightly toasted
10 g (⅓ oz) sesame seeds, lightly toasted
1 small handful herbs, such as parsley, chervil and thyme
1 small handful salad leaves

MOROCCAN WALLABY AND HARISSA SAUSAGE ROLLS

MAKES 8

Wallaby is available from many butchers and supermarkets in Australia. We choose it as a more sustainable meat option, being wild and abundant here. It's very lean and quite gamey and works beautifully with the harissa in this sausage roll. The harissa provides a gentle heat, there are little jewels of sweetness from the currants, and the almonds and couscous add variation in texture. If you don't have access to wallaby, then another game meat or lamb will work well here.

——

Put the couscous in a large bowl, pour over the boiling water and stir to combine. Cover with a clean cloth and set aside for 10 minutes. Put the currants in a small bowl, cover with water and set aside for 10 minutes. Roughly chop the toasted almonds.

Fluff up the couscous with a fork. Drain the currants and add them to the couscous along with the almonds, wallaby, harissa, milk, salt and pepper. Mix with your hands or a spoon, ensuring all the elements are evenly distributed. Transfer the mixture into a large piping bag with a 3 cm (1¼ in) diameter hole. (A piping bag will make it easier to distribute the filling, but you can always spoon it onto the pastry if you don't have one.) Refrigerate while you prepare the pastry.

Line a large baking tray with baking paper. Put the pastry on a lightly floured kitchen bench and roll it out into a rectangle measuring 30 × 60 cm (12 × 23½ in) and 4 mm (⅛ in) thick. Lay the pastry so that one long side is parallel with the edge of the bench. Cut the pastry in half lengthways so you have two sheets, 15 × 60 cm (6 × 23½ in).

Pipe half the filling in a horizontal line one-third of the way up each pastry sheet. Brush the pastry above each line of filling with egg wash. Lift up the pastry along the edge closest to you and fold it up and over the filling. Seal the pastry along the egg-washed edge, so the seam sits underneath the filling. The pastry should hold the filling evenly, and not be too tight.

Brush the tops and sides of both rolls with egg wash, lightly pierce along the top with a fork, then sprinkle the tops with sumac. Cut each roll into 15 cm (6 in) logs. Lay your sausage rolls on the lined tray and rest them in the fridge for 30 minutes. At this stage, you can freeze them until required.

To bake the sausage rolls, preheat the oven to 190°C (375°F). Bake from cold for 10 minutes, then reduce the oven to 180°C (360°F). Bake for a further 25–30 minutes, turning the tray halfway through, until the pastry is golden, puffed and flaky. Transfer to a wire rack to cool for 10 minutes before eating.

Pictured on page 172 (bottom).

80 g (2¾ oz) couscous
130 g (4½ oz) boiling water
80 g (2¾ oz) currants
65 g (2¼ oz) almonds, lightly toasted
800 g (1 lb 12 oz) minced (ground) wallaby
280 g (10 oz) Harissa (page 204)
55 g (2 oz) full-cream (whole) milk
6 g (⅕ oz/1 teaspoon) fine salt
3 g (¹⁄₁₀ oz/1¼ teaspoons) freshly ground black pepper
1 quantity Puff pastry (page 32)
Egg wash (page 15)
1 tablespoon sumac

PERSIAN LAMB SAUSAGE ROLLS

MAKES 8

These lamb sausage rolls combine many flavours and textures to pack a punch. There's the soft sweetness of sour cherries, the beautifully spiced lamb and the bite of pistachios all wrapped up in wonderfully flaky puff pastry. Since these are a bit more sophisticated than your average sausage roll, I often make bite-sized versions for entertaining.

———

40 g (1½ oz/2 tablespoons) olive oil
2 medium onions, finely chopped
4 garlic cloves, finely chopped
2 teaspoons ground turmeric
1 teaspoon ground cinnamon
1 tablespoon ground cumin
1 kg (2 lb 3 oz) minced (ground) lamb shoulder
50 g (1¾ oz) couscous
60 g (2 oz) pistachio nuts, roughly chopped
60 g (2 oz) dried sour cherries, roughly chopped
60 g (2 oz) pomegranate seeds
20 g (¾ oz/1 tablespoon) pomegranate molasses
grated zest and juice of 2 limes
2 tablespoons chopped parsley
2 tablespoons chopped coriander (cilantro) leaves
60 g (2 oz) plain (natural) yoghurt or full-cream (whole) milk, plus extra if needed
15 g (½ oz/2½ teaspoons) fine salt
1 quantity Puff pastry (page 32)
Egg wash (page 15)
1 tablespoon cumin seeds

Heat the olive oil in a frying pan over a medium heat. Fry the onion and garlic for 10–12 minutes until softened and starting to colour. Add the spices and cook for a further 2–3 minutes until fragrant. Set aside to cool.

In a large bowl, use clean hands to thoroughly combine the cooled onion mixture, lamb, couscous, pistachios, sour cherries, pomegranate seeds and molasses, lime zest and juice, herbs, yoghurt and salt. Transfer the mixture into a large piping bag with a 3 cm (1¼ in) diameter hole. (A piping bag will make it easier to distribute the filling, but you can always spoon it onto the pastry if you don't have one.) Refrigerate while you prepare the pastry.

Line a large baking tray with baking paper. Put the pastry on a lightly floured kitchen bench and roll it out into a rectangle measuring 30 × 60 cm (12 × 23½ in) and 4 mm (⅛ in) thick. Lay the pastry so that one long side is parallel with the edge of the bench. Cut the pastry in half lengthways so you have two sheets, 15 × 60 cm (6 × 23½ in).

Check the sausage mixture – the couscous and nuts may have absorbed more moisture. If the mix feels stiff, add 1–2 tablespoons yoghurt to loosen it a bit. Pipe half the filling in a horizontal line one-third of the way up each pastry sheet. Brush the pastry above each line of filling with egg wash. Lift up the pastry along the edge closest to you and fold it up and over the filling. Seal the pastry along the egg-washed edge, so the seam sits underneath the filling. The pastry should hold the filling evenly, and not be too tight.

Brush the tops and sides of both rolls with egg wash, lightly pierce along the top with a fork, then sprinkle the tops with cumin seeds. Cut each roll into 15 cm (6 in) logs, or smaller lengths if preferred. Lay your sausage rolls on the lined tray and rest them in the fridge for 30 minutes. At this stage, you can freeze them until required.

To bake the sausage rolls, preheat the oven to 190°C (375°F). Bake from cold for 10 minutes, then reduce the oven to 180°C (360°F). Bake for a further 25–30 minutes, turning the tray halfway through, until the pastry is golden, puffed and flaky. Transfer to a wire rack to cool for 10 minutes before eating.

Pictured on page 172 (top).

PORK, MISO AND SOYBEAN SAUSAGE ROLLS
MAKES 8

MAKE IT GLUTEN-FREE
Use gluten-free flaky pastry and breadcrumbs, substitute soy with tamari

Soy is a valuable source of protein, but unfortunately it is also one of the world's most intensively farmed, genetically modified crops – it's worth being selective about where you buy your soybeans and how they're grown. Always buy organic; they should be smooth and look clean. Soybeans do require soaking overnight in plenty of water, so you'll need to start this recipe a day in advance.

And it goes without saying that when selecting meat, you need to be vigilant about how the animals were reared and slaughtered. We buy our pork from Bundarra Berkshires in Barham, New South Wales. Lauren and Lachie Mathers raise healthy, happy pigs on their regenerative farm using biodynamic preparations on the soil and no antibiotics or chemicals of any kind. It's well worth getting to know your farmers so you can learn and understand how they farm, and the impacts of what they do on everything from the flavour and cost of your food to the environment.

Wakame marries well with the miso and ginger in these sausage rolls, adding a touch of salt and umami. You can find dried wakame in health food shops and Asian supermarkets – it also makes a delicious and healthy snack.

Heat the olive oil in a frying pan over a medium heat. Fry the onion for 10–12 minutes until softened and starting to colour. Stir in the ginger and garlic and cook for a further minute until fragrant. Set aside to cool.

In a small bowl, combine the miso, rice vinegar, honey, soy sauce, sesame oil and allspice, mixing thoroughly to ensure the miso and honey are fully incorporated.

Drain the soybeans and transfer to a large bowl. Add the cooled onion mixture, miso mixture, pork, spring onion, breadcrumbs and wakame. Mix with your hands or a spoon, ensuring all the elements are evenly distributed. Transfer the mixture into a large piping bag with a 3 cm (1¼ in) diameter hole. (A piping bag will make it easier to distribute the filling, but you can always spoon it onto the pastry if you don't have one.) Refrigerate while you prepare the pastry.

Line a large baking tray with baking paper. Put the pastry on a lightly floured kitchen bench and roll it out into a rectangle measuring 30 × 60 cm (12 × 23½ in) and 4 mm (⅛ in) thick. Lay the pastry so that one long side is parallel with the edge of the bench. Cut the pastry in half lengthways so you have two sheets, 15 × 60 cm (6 × 23½ in).

80 g (2¾ oz) olive oil
2 medium onions, finely chopped
60 g (2 oz) fresh ginger, grated
4 garlic cloves, finely chopped
60 g (2 oz) red miso paste
40 g (1½ oz/2 tablespoons) rice vinegar
25 g (1 oz/1 tablespoon) honey
1 tablespoon soy sauce
1 teaspoon sesame oil
¼ teaspoon ground allspice
60 g (2 oz) dried soybeans, soaked overnight in water
1 kg (2 lb 3 oz) minced (ground) pork
6 spring onions (scallions), trimmed and thinly sliced
150 g (5½ oz) dry breadcrumbs
10 g (⅓ oz) dried wakame
1 quantity Puff pastry (page 32)
Egg wash (page 15)
1 tablespoon sesame seeds

Pipe half the filling in a horizontal line one-third of the way up each pastry sheet. Brush the pastry above each line of filling with egg wash. Lift up the pastry along the edge closest to you and fold it up and over the filling. Seal the pastry along the egg-washed edge, so the seam sits underneath the filling. The pastry should hold the filling evenly, and not be too tight.

Brush the tops and sides of both rolls with egg wash, lightly pierce along the top with a fork, then sprinkle the tops with sesame seeds. Cut each roll into 15 cm (6 in) logs. Lay your sausage rolls on the lined tray and rest them in the fridge for 30 minutes. At this stage, you can freeze them until required.

To bake the sausage rolls, preheat the oven to 190°C (375°F). Bake from cold for 10 minutes, then reduce the oven to 180°C (360°F). Bake for a further 25–30 minutes, turning the tray halfway through, until the pastry is golden, puffed and flaky. Transfer to a wire rack to cool for 10 minutes before eating.

Pictured on page 173.

RABBIT AND WILD RICE PIE
SERVES 6-8

This gently spiced and wholesome dish is like a warm hug, and it is one of the tastiest pies I have ever had. The wild rice brings a lovely colour and texture, and there's a little kick of heat from the chilli – use a bit more if you like it hotter.

Don't be put off by the perceived effort required to cook with rabbit. Yes, there are lots of small bones. Braise it jointed as described here, after which the meat will fall easily from the bones. Alternatively, if you have a good butcher, ask them to debone it for you, reserving the bones so you can make a stock. If you don't have access to rabbit, substitute with chicken thighs.

Heat a large heavy-based saucepan or cast-iron casserole dish over a medium–high heat, then add a good knob of the butter and the olive oil. Brown the rabbit pieces in batches and set aside. Deglaze the pan with a little water or wine.

Reduce the heat to medium, then melt another knob of butter in the same pan. Add the onion and cook, stirring regularly, for 10–12 minutes until softened and golden. Add the garlic, chilli flakes, herbs and spices and cook for a further 2–3 minutes until fragrant.

Return the rabbit to the pan, add the stock and passata and stir to combine well. Bring to the boil, then reduce the heat to low, cover partially with the lid and simmer for 1 hour. Add the wild rice and simmer for a further 30 minutes. Remove the rabbit pieces and increase the heat to reduce the sauce by half.

When the rabbit is cool enough to handle, pick the meat off the bones, being very careful not to miss any small bones. (You can keep the bones to roast and make a stock for your next pie.) Dice any larger pieces of meat, then mix it all back through the sauce. Season to taste with salt and pepper. Refrigerate for a few hours or overnight before assembling and baking your pie(s) (see page 22).

The pictured pie was made using plain flaky shortcrust pastry for the top.

60 g (2 oz) unsalted butter

30 g (1 oz/1½ tablespoons) olive oil

1 rabbit (approx. 1.5 kg/3 lb 5 oz), jointed

water or wine, for deglazing

2 medium onions, roughly chopped

4 garlic cloves, finely chopped

½ teaspoon chilli flakes

4 rosemary sprigs, leaves picked and chopped

4 thyme sprigs, leaves picked

1 teaspoon cumin seeds

1 teaspoon fennel seeds

1 litre (34 fl oz) rabbit, chicken or vegetable stock

300 g (10½ oz) tomato passata or chopped tomatoes

200 g (7 oz) wild rice

fine salt

freshly ground black pepper

pastry of choice (see Pie basics, page 22)

THAI GREEN CURRY SAUSAGE ROLLS

MAKES 8

MAKE IT GLUTEN-FREE
Use gluten-free flaky pastry

Thai is one of my favourite cuisines to cook at home, and this is my twist on a much-loved classic.

For a juicy, tender and flavoursome sausage roll, I prefer to use chicken thigh meat. It tastes great after baking and doesn't dry out as much as breast meat. If you're planning ahead, refrigerate the mixture for a day or two to let the spices and herbs marinate the chicken. If not, it will still be delicious. If you like a bit of heat, leave the seeds in when chopping the chillies.

———

Heat the olive oil in a frying pan over a medium heat. Fry the onion and garlic for 10–12 minutes until softened and starting to colour. Add the lemongrass, chilli and curry paste and cook for a few minutes until fragrant. Set aside to cool.

In a large bowl, combine the cooled onion mixture, chicken, kaffir lime leaves, herbs, fish sauce and coconut. Mix with your hands or a wooden spoon, ensuring all the elements are evenly distributed through the chicken. Transfer the mixture into a large piping bag with a 3 cm (1¼ in) diameter hole. (A piping bag will make it easier to distribute the filling, but you can always spoon it onto the pastry if you don't have one.) Refrigerate while you prepare the pastry.

Line a large baking tray with baking paper. Put the pastry on a floured kitchen bench and roll it out into a rectangle measuring 30 × 60 cm (12 × 23½ in) and 4 mm (⅛ in) thick. Lay the pastry so that one long side is parallel with the edge of the bench. Cut the pastry in half lengthways so you have two sheets, 15 × 60 cm (6 × 23½ in).

Pipe half the filling in a horizontal line one-third of the way up each pastry sheet. Brush the pastry above each line of filling with egg wash. Lift up the pastry along the edge closest to you and fold it up and over the filling. Seal the pastry along the egg-washed edge, so the seam sits underneath the filling. The pastry should hold the filling evenly, and not be too tight.

Brush the tops and sides of both rolls with egg wash, lightly pierce along the top with a fork, then sprinkle the tops with sesame seeds. Cut each roll into 15 cm (6 in) logs. Lay your sausage rolls on the lined tray and rest them in the fridge for 30 minutes. At this stage, you can freeze them until required.

To bake the sausage rolls, preheat the oven to 190°C (375°F). Bake from cold for 10 minutes, then reduce the oven to 180°C (360°F). Bake for a further 25–30 minutes, turning the tray halfway through, until the pastry is golden, puffed and flaky. Transfer to a wire rack to cool for 10 minutes before eating.

40 g (1½ oz/2 tablespoons) olive oil
2 medium onions, finely chopped
4 garlic cloves, finely chopped
2 teaspoons finely chopped lemongrass, white part only
2 green chillies, finely chopped
140 g (5 oz) green curry paste
1 kg (2 lb 3 oz) boneless, skinless chicken thighs, coarsely minced
4 kaffir lime leaves, thinly sliced
2 tablespoons chopped coriander (cilantro) leaves
2 tablespoons chopped Thai basil
20 g (¾ oz/1 tablespoon) fish sauce
30 g (1 oz) desiccated (fine) coconut
1 quantity Puff pastry (page 32)
Egg wash (page 15)
1 tablespoon sesame seeds

CAULIFLOWER AND ALMOND CHEESE PIE
SERVES 6-8

This is my version of the classic cauliflower cheese but in pie form. It's the ultimate comfort food and a simple way to make vegetables the centre of a meal. I like to add roasted almonds with the skin on, for extra texture and flavour.

For variation, try a combination of cauliflower and broccoli, or chop up some dark leafy greens and stir them through the sauce.

—

2 small or 1 large (approx. 900 g/ 2 lb) cauliflower
50 g (1¾ oz) unsalted butter
2 large onions, chopped
4 garlic cloves, finely chopped
1 tablespoon finely chopped rosemary
1 tablespoon finely chopped sage
100 g (3½ oz) almonds, roughly chopped
juice of 1 lemon
pastry of choice (see Pie basics, page 22)

BÉCHAMEL
600 g (1 lb 5 oz) full-cream (whole) milk
3 cloves
2 fresh bay leaves
½ teaspoon freshly grated nutmeg
60 g (2 oz) unsalted butter
60 g (2 oz) plain (all-purpose) flour
20 g (¾ oz/1 tablespoon) Wholegrain mustard (page 211)
12 g (½ oz/2 teaspoons) fine salt
200 g (7 oz) cheddar, grated
100 g (3½ oz) parmesan, grated

Bring a large saucepan of salted water to the boil. Cut the cauliflower into large florets and blanch in the boiling water for 2 minutes. Drain well and leave to cool.

Meanwhile, melt the butter in a heavy-based frying pan over a medium heat. Fry the onion and garlic for 8–10 minutes until soft and translucent. Stir in the rosemary and sage, then remove from the heat and leave to cool.

To make the béchamel, warm the milk with the cloves, bay leaves and nutmeg in a small saucepan over a low heat, ensuring it doesn't come to the boil. Strain and discard the aromats.

Melt the butter in a medium saucepan over a medium heat. Add the flour and whisk to combine. Cook, whisking, for 4–5 minutes until the mixture darkens slightly and resembles sand. Slowly add the warm milk in three additions, whisking as you go to get rid of any lumps. Bring to a simmer over a low heat for 2–3 minutes until the sauce thickens. Add the mustard, salt and cheeses and stir through until well combined. Set aside to cool.

Combine the cauliflower, onion mixture, almonds and lemon juice in a large bowl. Pour over the béchamel and stir it through so everything is coated. Check for seasoning and add more salt or mustard, to taste. Refrigerate for a few hours or overnight before assembling and baking your pie(s) (see page 22).

BUTTER CHICKEN PIE
SERVES 6

Since leaving London, we miss the great Indian restaurants, so now we tend to cook a lot of Indian food at home. I also make a big batch of Fermented lime pickle (page 206) each winter, which is great with this pie, as is Tomato kasundi (page 205). This recipe does look like a bit of effort, with two marinades plus a sauce, but each step is simple, so please don't be discouraged. I like to use macadamias – they're so sweet and meaty – but cashews or peanuts would also work well. A heavy cast-iron pan is great for cooking the chicken, as it gives a lovely heat and colour.

DAY 1

To prepare the first marinade, combine the lime juice and chilli powder in a large bowl. Add the chicken and toss to coat. Cover and refrigerate for 2 hours.

To prepare the second marinade, put all the ingredients in a bowl and stir to combine well. Add this to the chicken and mix well so the chicken is fully coated. Cover and refrigerate overnight.

DAY 2

Take the chicken out of the fridge and bring to room temperature. Heat a cast-iron or heavy-based frying pan over a medium–high heat. Brown the chicken in batches until golden but not cooked through. Remove from the pan and set aside.

To make the sauce, dry-roast the coriander and cumin seeds in a small frying pan over a medium heat for 1 minute, or until fragrant. Grind the spices and set aside.

Melt the ghee in a large heavy-based saucepan or cast-iron casserole dish over a medium heat. Add the garlic and ginger and cook for 1–2 minutes until fragrant. Add the tomatoes and bring to a slow simmer for 5 minutes. Add all the spices, coconut and salt and simmer over a low heat for a further 10 minutes, then add the chicken pieces and simmer for 10 minutes, or until the chicken is just cooked through. Add a little water to loosen the sauce if required. Remove the pan from the heat and stir through the macadamias, cream and coriander. Refrigerate for a few hours or overnight before assembling and baking your pie(s) (see page 22).

Pictured on page 182, top left. The pie was made using plain flaky shortcrust pastry for the top. It was garnished with nigella seeds.

750 g (1 lb 11 oz) boneless, skinless chicken thighs, cut into 2 cm (¾ in) dice
pastry of choice (see Pie basics, page 22)

FIRST MARINADE
juice of 2 limes
1 teaspoon chilli powder

SECOND MARINADE
50 g (1¾ oz) plain (natural) yoghurt
50 g (1¾ oz) cream
5 garlic cloves, roughly chopped
5 cm (2 in) piece fresh ginger, roughly chopped
1 teaspoon garam masala
1 teaspoon ground turmeric
1 teaspoon ground cumin

SAUCE
1 teaspoon coriander seeds
1 teaspoon cumin seeds
50 g (1¾ oz) ghee or butter
5 garlic cloves, finely crushed
5 cm (2 in) piece fresh ginger, finely grated
1 × 400 g (14 oz) tin chopped tomatoes
½ teaspoon chilli powder
½ teaspoon ground cinnamon
½ teaspoon garam masala
1 teaspoon desiccated (fine) coconut
1½ teaspoons fine salt
100 g (3½ oz) macadamia nuts, lightly toasted and chopped
50 g (1¾ oz) cream
½ bunch coriander (cilantro), leaves and stems chopped

EASY TO ADAPT
MAKE IT VEGAN
*Use vegan flaky pastry, use oil instead
of butter, use coconut yoghurt*

INDIAN VEGETABLE CURRY PIE
SERVES 6

I grew up in Cornwall and lived next door to an Indian family. They cooked the most amazing food and sometimes would bring it over to share with us. This was such a joyful experience for me.

I call this my 'use-up' curry – it's perfect for making good use of whatever vegetables you have in the fridge. Topped with puff or flaky shortcrust pastry, it makes the most delicious, full-flavoured curry pie, and, for me, it brings back memories of all the wonderful smells and the taste of my neighbours' food. This pie also goes well with Fermented lime pickle (page 206) or Tomato kasundi (page 205).

---

900 g (2 lb) mixed vegetables, such as sweet potato, carrot, capsicum (bell pepper), eggplant (aubergine), cauliflower, green beans, peas, leeks
olive oil, for frying
pastry of choice (see Pie basics, page 22)

SAUCE
50 g (1¾ oz) ghee or butter
1 large onion, sliced
6 garlic cloves
30 g (1 oz) fresh ginger, chopped
10 g (⅓ oz) fresh turmeric, chopped, or 1 teaspoon ground turmeric
1 teaspoon chilli powder
½ teaspoon ground coriander
½ teaspoon ground cumin
½ teaspoon ground cinnamon
½ teaspoon garam masala
1 tablespoon desiccated (fine) coconut
1½ teaspoons fine salt
400 g (14 oz) tomato passata or 1 × 400 g (14 oz) tin chopped tomatoes
240 g (8½ oz) water
30 g (1 oz) cashew nuts
100 g (3½ oz) plain (natural) yoghurt
juice of 1 lemon or lime
½ bunch coriander (cilantro), leaves roughly chopped

Chop your larger vegetables, such as root vegetables and cauliflower, into bite-sized pieces – about 2–3 cm (1½–2 in). Roughly chop your smaller vegetables, such as beans and leeks. Bring a large saucepan of salted water to the boil and blanch the harder vegetables, such as carrots, sweet potato or cauliflower, just enough to take the crunch off and make them a little tender. Drain well.

If you're using leek, eggplant or other softer vegetables that benefit from longer heat, cook them with a little olive oil in a frying pan over a medium heat for about 5 minutes to lightly colour and soften them, then set aside. Vegetables such as beans or peas can remain raw at this stage.

To make the sauce, melt the ghee in a large heavy-based saucepan over a medium heat. Fry the onion for 10–12 minutes until softened and golden on the edges. Add the garlic, ginger and turmeric and fry for 1 minute, or until fragrant. Add the spices, coconut and salt and fry for a further minute until fragrant, then add the passata and 100 g (3½ oz) of the water. Bring to the boil, then reduce the heat to low and simmer for 10 minutes.

Meanwhile, put the cashews and 40 g (1½ oz/2 tablespoons) water in a small food processor and process to a paste. Alternatively, use a mortar and pestle to do this. Stir the cashew paste into the sauce.

Add all your vegetables to the pan with the remaining 100 g (3½ oz) water and bring to a simmer, then remove from the heat and leave to cool a little. Stir in the yoghurt, lemon juice and coriander. Refrigerate for a few hours or overnight before assembling and baking your pie(s) (see page 22).

Pictured on page 182, top right. The pie was made using shortcrust pastry for the base and wholemeal puff pastry for the top.

KANGAROO, MUSHROOM AND ALE PIE

SERVES 4-6

Like many people, we're on a mission to tread more lightly on Earth. In Australia, kangaroos are wild and plentiful, and one of the most sustainable meats we have access to. It is now widely accepted that the general level of consumption of red meat, particularly beef, is a major factor in our climate crisis. In Australia there is an extra layer of complexity because of the damage that hooved animals have caused to the soft, ancient soils. We do still eat a small amount of beef, always from farmers that we know are caring for their land and their animals.

This is a classic mushroom and ale pie, a pub favourite, hearty and deep flavoured thanks to the dark ale. Kangaroo is really lean, which is why we don't cook it for hours. Chunks of mushroom enhance the texture; we forage wonderful pine mushrooms each autumn just outside Melbourne. They're a toothsome and flavourful seasonal treat, perfect for this rich and tasty pie, although you can use king oyster, field or other large mushrooms instead.

Heat a large heavy-based saucepan or cast-iron casserole dish over a medium–high heat and melt 25 g (1 oz) of the butter. Brown the kangaroo in batches, then remove from the pan.

Return the pan to a medium heat and melt the remaining 25 g (1 oz) butter. Add the onion and cook with the lid on, stirring occasionally, for 10–12 minutes until golden and translucent. Add the garlic and cook for 1 minute, or until fragrant. Add the mushrooms and thyme and stir well to combine. Cook for a further 5–8 minutes until the mushrooms start to soften.

Add the kangaroo, ale and bay leaves and stir to combine. Bring to the boil, then reduce the heat to low and simmer for 30 minutes. Strain the liquid into a small saucepan and bring to the boil to reduce by one-third. Mix the cornflour with a little water to make a slurry, then stir it through the sauce to thicken slightly before pouring it back over the kangaroo. Season to taste with salt and pepper. Refrigerate for a few hours or overnight before assembling and baking your pie(s) (see page 22).

Pictured on page 183. The pie was made using plain puff pastry for the top.

50 g (1¾ oz) unsalted butter
550 g (1 lb 3 oz) kangaroo fillet, cut into 1 cm (½ in) dice
2 medium onions, roughly chopped
4 garlic cloves, finely chopped
550 g (1 lb 3 oz) mushrooms, sliced or roughly torn
10 thyme sprigs, leaves picked
330 g (11½ oz) dark ale
4 fresh bay leaves
15 g (½ oz/3 teaspoons) cornflour (cornstarch)
fine salt
freshly ground black pepper
pastry of choice (see Pie basics, page 22)

KANGAROO, SWEET POTATO, PRUNE AND PRESERVED LEMON PIE
SERVES 4-6

Being a strongly flavoured meat, kangaroo is great with the sweetness of the potato and prunes here. We always preserve any lemons we can get our hands on in winter, and love them as a piquant seasoning for dishes cooked throughout the year. The lemon is pickled in salt and, over time, the sourness softens, leaving a salty, bright ferment that cuts through the rich flavours in this pie filling. You can also substitute kangaroo with beef, lamb or chicken.

———

½ cinnamon stick
1 teaspoon cumin seeds
1 teaspoon coriander seeds
4 cardamom pods
1 teaspoon ground turmeric
65 g (2¼ oz) olive oil
500 g (1 lb 2 oz) kangaroo fillet, cut into 1–2 cm (½–¾ in) dice
50 g (1¾ oz) unsalted butter
1 large onion, roughly chopped
4 garlic cloves, finely chopped
5 cm (2 in) piece fresh ginger, finely chopped
600 g (1 lb 5 oz) sweet potatoes, peeled and cut into 1–2 cm (½–¾ in) dice
400 g (14 oz) chicken stock
2 fresh bay leaves
3 thyme sprigs, leaves picked
100 g (3½ oz) pitted prunes, roughly chopped
30 g (1 oz) Preserved lemon rind, finely chopped (page 192)
fine salt
freshly ground black pepper
pastry of choice (see Pie basics, page 22)

Put the cinnamon, cumin, coriander and cardamom in a frying pan over a medium heat and dry-roast for 1–2 minutes until fragrant. Remove from the pan and crush using a mortar and pestle, discarding the outer layer of the cardamom pods.

Combine the crushed spices with the turmeric and 40 g (1½ oz/ 2 tablespoons) of the olive oil in a medium bowl and stir to create a paste. Add the kangaroo and stir it through to ensure the meat is thoroughly coated. Refrigerate for 2 hours, or overnight.

Heat a large heavy-based saucepan or cast-iron casserole dish over a medium–high heat and melt 25 g (1 oz) of the butter. Brown the kangaroo in batches, then remove from the pan.

Return the pan to a medium heat and melt the remaining 25 g (1 oz) butter and 25 g (1 oz) olive oil. Add the onion, garlic and ginger and cook with the lid on, stirring occasionally, for 10–12 minutes until golden and translucent.

Add the kangaroo and sweet potato and stir to combine. Add the stock, bay leaves, thyme, prunes and preserved lemon. Bring to the boil, then reduce the heat to low and simmer for 30 minutes. Season to taste with salt and pepper. Refrigerate for a few hours or overnight before assembling and baking your pie(s) (see page 22).

UNWAXED
LEMONS

PANTRY

14 PERFECT COMPLEMENTS
PAGES 188–213

PUMPKIN

PANTRY

This is a fun and interesting chapter. Making pantry staples that are usually bought in bottles in a supermarket is an excellent way to use what is around you. Preserving is a way of life that predates refrigeration and is really the ultimate in seasonal and sustainable eating – buying or picking a glut of fruit at its peak and preserving it for year-round enjoyment and diverting potential food waste. It's extremely rewarding to transform simple ingredients into something that is more than the sum of their parts. Take sauerkraut, for example. With a little creativity, cabbage, salt and a few spices can become an indispensable addition to your table.

I hope you will appreciate the extra flavour and nutrition gained by eating real ingredients rather than industrially farmed, factory-processed products. In the ketchups and chutneys, the natural sweetness gained by using fruit at its peak means that little or no added sugar is needed. Ripeness is important here.

Have fun with the hot sauce; watch it ferment and expand. Play around with the mustard to find just the right level of heat for you. Go foraging in the weeds for nasturtium seed pods and never buy expensive capers from the fancy deli again.

Unless you know the condiment will be eaten quickly, always sterilise your jars to properly preserve what you've made – preserves will last almost indefinitely in sterilised containers. To sterilise your jars, preheat the oven to 120°C (250°F). Wash them in hot soapy water and rinse thoroughly, then place them in the oven for 20 minutes. Make sure your jars are completely dry and still warm when you fill them.

All of the preserves in this chapter will benefit from time once completed – keep them at room temperature and out of direct sunlight while they are maturing. The longer they sit, the more delicious and complex they become. Vinegars will mellow and flavours will change and mature over time. And of course, any of the recipes here make the best type of gift: a homemade one.

PRESERVED LEMONS
FILLS 4 × 300 ML (10 FL OZ) JARS

Lemons grow in abundance where we live. A few years ago, we had a particularly big glut and I was wondering what to do with them all. The obvious thing was to preserve them so they are on hand for months, or even years, ahead. We recently finished off a jar from that year and it was so good – umami, salty, acidic, mellow and sour all at once.

We use preserved lemon a lot. The pulp and skin are useful in the kitchen added to all sorts of things, such as salads, sauces, mayonnaise and braises. The juice will thicken over time and is wonderful in dressings or simply mixed with a little olive oil over pasta.

This is a wonderful introduction to preserving. You need just two main ingredients – lemon and salt – plus whatever herbs and spices are around at the time. The list below is a guide; I've also used cinnamon sticks, cardamom pods and juniper berries with success. The other hidden ingredient is, of course, time; this is lacto-fermentation. It will take six weeks until you can start to use the lemons, although they are even better if left for two to three months.

You can do this with limes, oranges or other citrus fruits. A good tip is to freeze the quarters overnight before preserving, as this softens the skin and helps to speed up the process.

———

Quarter the lemons and remove the pips (this is not essential). Put the lemons in a large bowl and add the salt. Massage the salt firmly into the lemons until it is well mixed and juice is coming out of the lemons. Add the herbs, peppercorns and cloves and mix through evenly. Set aside while you sterilise your jars (see page 188).

Press down hard on the lemons to release as much juice as possible, then transfer to your sterilised jars. Start by placing some of the salt mixture in the bottom of the jar. Pack the lemons in tightly, with the rind of each piece against the glass and the flesh facing in. Add the herbs and spices as you go, so they are well dispersed and not in a layer at the top of the jar. Top up each jar with the salty juice you squeezed from the lemons, pushing down at the end. The fruit needs to be completely covered in juice; if you don't have enough, add extra juice to cover. Wipe off any juices from the sides and seal the jars.

Leave to ferment at room temperature for 6 weeks, turning the jars upside down once a week or so to help disperse the salt and flavourings. The lemons are ready when the salt has completely dissolved, the rind is more translucent and the liquid is gel-like. They will keep for years in the fridge once opened, with the flavours developing more and more over time.

To use the preserved lemon, remove from the jar, scrape away the bay leaves, pips and spices, cut finely, then use as directed.

10 medium unwaxed lemons
300 g (10½ oz) coarse sea salt
2–3 fresh bay leaves, torn
2–3 thyme sprigs
2–3 rosemary sprigs
10 whole black peppercorns
2–3 whole cloves

TOMATO KETCHUP

FILLS 2 × 300 ML (10 FL OZ) JARS

Commercial ketchups are laden with sugar and salt; here is a version you can feel better about giving to your kids. It uses fruit and vegetables at their prime for sun-ripened sweetness and real flavour. Make it at the cusp of autumn when tomatoes are at their best and the first crunchy apples of the season are just coming in.

———

Bring a large saucepan of water to the boil, and fill a large bowl with ice and water. Blanch the tomatoes in the pan of boiling water for 10–20 seconds, then plunge them into the iced water. Peel and roughly chop the tomatoes and transfer to a bowl. Mix the salt through, then transfer the tomatoes to a colander set over a bowl. Set aside for at least 3 hours to allow the excess water to release. Discard the drained tomato liquid or set aside for another use. I like to use it as a simple stock for soups or risottos.

Make the spice bag by laying the ingredients on a square of muslin (cheesecloth), then tie it up to enclose them.

Put the tomato, spice bag, chopped apple and vegetables and all the remaining ingredients in a large heavy-based saucepan over a medium heat. Bring to a slow boil, stirring occasionally, then reduce the heat to low and simmer for 1 hour, or until reduced by about one-third. Cool slightly, then remove the spice bag and squeeze out the juices into the pan.

Transfer to a food processor and blitz to form a smooth purée. Return the purée to the pan and bring to the boil, then simmer over a low heat for 20 minutes, or until it thickens to a nice consistency. Sterilise your jars while the ketchup cools (see page 188).

Pour the ketchup into the sterilised jars and seal. Leave for at least 2 weeks before using, to allow the flavours to marry and the sharpness of the vinegar to subside. Store the unopened jars in the pantry for up to 1 year. Refrigerate after opening and use within 1 month.

Pictured on page 196.

900 g (2 lb) ripe tomatoes
10 g (⅓ oz) flaky sea salt
spice bag: 1 fresh bay leaf,
    1 teaspoon celery seeds,
    ½ teaspoon whole black
    peppercorns, ½ teaspoon
    whole cloves
200 g (7 oz) crisp eating apples,
    such as braeburn or fuji,
    peeled and roughly chopped
200 g (7 oz) red onions, roughly
    chopped
2 red capsicums (bell peppers),
    seeded and roughly chopped
1 garlic clove, roughly chopped
1 teaspoon sweet paprika
½ teaspoon ground allspice
¼ teaspoon cayenne pepper
120 g (4½ oz) raw (demerara)
    sugar
150 g (5½ oz) apple-cider
    vinegar

PUMPKIN KETCHUP

FILLS 3 × 300 ML (10 FL OZ) JARS

The first ketchup was made with mushrooms, and many different vegetables were used before the ubiquitous tomato version became so prevalent.

I first made this pumpkin ketchup to complement the Mushroom, rye and preserved lemon pithiviers (page 160). Pumpkins and mushrooms are both reaped in autumn and pair beautifully. Here, the pumpkin gives sweetness and texture that, with a little kick from the spices, go really well with a lot of savoury bakes. I find butternut pumpkin works well, though you can use any kind of pumpkin.

---

spice bag: 1 fresh bay leaf, 1 cinnamon stick, ¼ lime, ¼ teaspoon whole cloves, ¼ teaspoon celery seeds, ¼ teaspoon chilli flakes
30 g (1 oz/1½ tablespoons) olive oil
1 medium onion, roughly chopped
1 red capsicum (bell pepper), seeded and roughly chopped
1 garlic clove, chopped
500 g (1 lb 2 oz) butternut pumpkin (squash), peeled and roughly chopped
100 g (3½ oz) white-wine vinegar
50 g (1¾ oz) apple-cider vinegar
100 g (3½ oz) water
50 g (1¾ oz) raw (demerara) sugar
10 g (⅓ oz) flaky sea salt
½ teaspoon ground turmeric
½ teaspoon ground ginger
½ teaspoon cayenne pepper
¼ teaspoon ground nutmeg

Make the spice bag by laying the ingredients on a square of muslin (cheesecloth), then tie it up to enclose them.

Heat the olive oil in a large heavy-based saucepan over a medium–low heat. Add the onion, capsicum and garlic and cook with the lid on, stirring occasionally, for 10–15 minutes until softened.

Add the spice bag and all remaining ingredients to the pan. Bring to the boil, then reduce the heat to low. Cover and simmer, stirring occasionally, for 30–40 minutes until the pumpkin is completely soft. Cool slightly, then remove the spice bag and squeeze out the juices into the pan.

Transfer to a food processor and blitz for 2–3 minutes to form a smooth purée. Return the purée to the pan over a low–medium heat and cook for a further 30–40 minutes until it reaches your desired consistency. Sterilise your jars while the ketchup cools (see page 188).

Pour the ketchup into the sterilised jars and seal. Leave for at least 2 weeks before using, to allow the flavours to marry and the sharpness of the vinegar to subside. Store the unopened jars in the pantry for up to 1 year. Refrigerate after opening and use within 1 month.

Pictured on page 196.

BROWN SAUCE

FILLS 3 × 300 ML (10 FL OZ) JARS

Brown sauce is a classic British condiment, excellent with a range of things from pork pies to a sausage sandwich. Commercial versions are loaded with sugar, but here the apples, prunes and dates give it a natural sweetness.

This can be mouth-puckeringly acidic when you first taste it, but after a few weeks the vinegar will mellow and you'll get this fantastic classic sauce that you made all yourself.

In a large heavy-based saucepan, combine the apple, onion, garlic, dates, prunes, water, white-wine vinegar, fruit juices, tomato paste, tamarind and treacle. Cover and bring to the boil over a medium heat. Reduce the heat to low, then take the lid off and cook for about 40 minutes, or until the apple and onion are soft.

Meanwhile, use a spice grinder or mortar and pestle to grind the mustard seeds and peppercorns to a fine powder. Combine the ground seeds with the remaining spices and salt. Add the rye flour and apple-cider vinegar and mix well.

Remove the pan from the heat and cool a little, then transfer to a food processor and blitz to form a smooth purée. Return the purée to the pan over a medium heat and slowly bring to the boil. Reduce to a simmer, then stir in the spice and vinegar mixture. Continue to simmer over a low heat, stirring occasionally, for a further 40 minutes, or until you are happy with the consistency. Sterilise your jars while the sauce cools (see page 188).

Transfer the brown sauce into the sterilised jars and seal. Leave for at least 2–4 weeks before using, to allow the sharpness of the vinegar to subside. Store the unopened jars in the pantry for up to 1 year. Refrigerate after opening and use within 1 month.

Pictured on page 197.

400 g (14 oz) crisp eating apples, such as braeburn or fuji, peeled and roughly chopped
200 g (7 oz) red onions, roughly chopped
1 garlic clove, sliced
50 g (1¾ oz) pitted dates, chopped
35 g (1¼ oz) pitted prunes, chopped
100 g (3½ oz) water
250 g (9 oz) white-wine vinegar
120 g (4½ oz) apple juice
120 g (4½ oz) orange juice
125 g (4½ oz) tomato paste (concentrated purée)
150 g (5½ oz) tamarind purée
25 g (1 oz) black treacle or molasses
¼ teaspoon brown mustard seeds
¼ teaspoon whole black peppercorns
¼ teaspoon ground cloves
¼ teaspoon ground cardamom
¼ teaspoon ground cinnamon
¼ teaspoon onion powder
¼ teaspoon cayenne pepper
½ teaspoon ground allspice
½ teaspoon fine salt
20 g (¾ oz) rye flour
75 g (2¾ oz) apple-cider vinegar

GREEN TOMATO AND TARRAGON RELISH

FILLS 3 × 300 ML (10 FL OZ) JARS

Green tomatoes are early autumn's gift to preservers. In that transitional time when the nights are getting cooler, there is often still plenty of fruit on the vines that just will not ripen. The best thing to do is use them up, and this vibrant green relish is a wonderful way to do so. Use it with hot dogs, with a quiche, in a sandwich, or with cheeseburgers.

---

800 g (1 lb 12 oz) green tomatoes, cut into 1 cm (½ in) pieces
20 g (¾ oz) fine salt
70 g (2½ oz) olive oil
50 g (1¾ oz) fresh ginger, finely grated
1 garlic clove, finely chopped
2 fresh bay leaves
1 teaspoon yellow mustard seeds
½ teaspoon ground coriander seeds
½ teaspoon ground fenugreek
¼ teaspoon freshly ground black pepper
¼ teaspoon ground turmeric
500 g (1 lb 2 oz) onions, thinly sliced
50 g (1¾ oz) raw (demerara) sugar
200 g (7 oz) white-wine vinegar
2 tarragon sprigs, leaves picked and finely chopped

Combine the chopped tomatoes and salt in a colander set over a bowl. Set aside for at least 1 hour to allow the excess water to release.

Heat the olive oil in a large heavy-based saucepan over a medium heat. Add the ginger, garlic, bay leaves and spices and toast until fragrant. Add the onion and cook with the lid on, stirring occasionally, for about 15 minutes, or until softened.

Add the drained tomatoes to the pan and mix well. Add the sugar and vinegar, stirring to dissolve. Slowly bring to the boil, then reduce the heat to low and simmer for about 40 minutes, or until the mixture is shiny and thick with no excess liquid. Cool slightly and check the seasoning, adding more salt to taste if necessary. Stir through the tarragon. Sterilise your jars while the relish cools (see page 188).

Spoon the relish into the sterilised jars and seal. Store the unopened jars in the pantry for up to 1 year. Refrigerate after opening and use within 1 month.

Pictured on page 197.

CARAMELISED ONION AND APPLE CHUTNEY
FILLS 3 × 300 ML (10 FL OZ) JARS

This is similar in taste to a branston pickle, but much simpler. I make up a big batch of this about once a year, and the flavour just keeps on improving as time goes by. It's great with a sausage roll or in a sandwich with really bitey cheddar.

———

Make the spice bag by laying the ingredients on a square of muslin (cheesecloth), then tie it up to enclose them.

Heat the olive oil in a large heavy-based saucepan over a low heat. Add the onion and salt and cook with the lid on, stirring occasionally, for 10–15 minutes until softened and transparent.

Stir in the sugar and chilli flakes and cook for 2–3 minutes with the lid off, then add the apple, vinegars and spice bag. Slowly bring to the boil, then reduce the heat to low and simmer for a further 45 minutes, or until the liquid is reduced and the mixture is glossy and thick. Remove the pan from the heat and cool for 10 minutes, then remove the spice bag and squeeze out the juices into the pan. Sterilise your jars while the chutney cools (see page 188).

Spoon the chutney into the sterilised jars and seal. Leave for at least 2 weeks before using, to allow the flavours to marry and the sharpness of the vinegar to subside. Store the unopened jars in the pantry for up to 1 year. Refrigerate after opening and use within 1 month.

spice bag: 2 fresh bay leaves, ½ lime, 1 teaspoon brown mustard seeds, 1 teaspoon cumin seeds, 1 teaspoon black peppercorns
20 g (¾ oz/1 tablespoon) olive oil
900 g (2 lb) red onions, thinly sliced
6 g (⅕ oz/1 teaspoon) fine salt
200 g (7 oz) dark brown sugar
½ teaspoon chilli flakes
380 g (13½ oz) crisp eating apples, such as braeburn or fuji, peeled and roughly chopped
200 g (7 oz) balsamic vinegar
75 g (2¾ oz) apple-cider vinegar

HABANERO AND MANGO HOT SAUCE

FILLS 2 × 250 ML (8½ FL OZ) JARS

I had no idea how simple this was, but once I'd made it, I wondered why I'd never done it before. Now I use it in lots of ways: mixed into mayonnaise with fried chicken; added to braises, salsas or guacamole; a few drops in an extra spicy bloody mary; or for a kick in salad dressings. Just remember, this hot sauce does what it says on the label – a little goes a long way.

I use habaneros, as they have a good kick but not the extreme heat of some other chillies. They have a great aroma, too. You can use green jalapeños if you like. The fruit adds body to the sauce and a touch of sweetness. I love using mango when it's in season, but pineapple, peach or lychee are also good.

To make it more of a sriracha-style sauce, add 1 tablespoon raw (demerara) sugar and an extra 100 g (3½ oz) vinegar when you purée the mixture after fermenting.

———

400 g (14 oz) habanero chillies
approx. 7 g (¼ oz) flaky sea salt
    (or 1.75% of chilli weight after
    chopping)
approx. 100 g (3½ oz) mango
    flesh (or 25% of chilli weight)
1 garlic clove
30 g (1 oz/1½ tablespoons)
    apple-cider vinegar

Remove the stalks from the chillies and discard. Finely chop the chillies and then weigh the chopped amount. Calculate 1.75% of this weight; this is the exact weight for your salt. Weigh and add the salt, then mix it through the chilli. Calculate 25% of the chilli weight; this is the weight for your mango. Chop the mango and garlic, then mix them through the chilli.

Transfer the mixture into a large jar with enough space for the chilli mixture to expand as it ferments. Leave to ferment for at least 7 days, giving it a good stir once a day. By day 4, you should start to see bubbles. By day 7 or 8, you should see bubbles throughout the chilli and on top. At this point, sterilise your jars (see page 188).

Add the vinegar to the chilli ferment, then transfer to a food processor and blitz until you have a smooth purée. Pour the sauce into the sterilised jars and seal them. Put the jars in a saucepan of boiling water (the water should come up to just below the lids), then reduce the heat to low and simmer for 10 minutes. This stops the fermentation and makes the sauce shelf-stable, but also removes the probiotic benefits from the ferment.

Store the unopened jars in the pantry for 2 years (the flavour will improve over time). Refrigerate after opening and use within 6 months. This sauce is all natural with no stabilisers, so you may need to give the jar a shake before use.

HARISSA
FILLS 3 × 300 ML (10 FL OZ) JARS

Having a jar of harissa in the fridge is like money in the bank. It can be used in so many ways to provide warm spice and interest to different dishes. I love it with eggs for breakfast, with roasted vegetables for a midweek dinner, or mixed with yoghurt for a milder condiment.

———

Roast the capsicums under a hot grill (broiler) or over an open flame until they are black and blistered. Set aside to cool, then peel off the charred skins and remove the stems and seeds.

Heat the olive oil in a large saucepan over a medium–low heat. Add the onion and cook, stirring occasionally, for about 20 minutes, or until softened and golden. Add the garlic and chilli and cook for 1–2 minutes to release the fragrance.

Meanwhile, dry-roast the coriander, cumin and fennel seeds in a small frying pan over a low heat until fragrant. Use a spice grinder or mortar and pestle to grind the spices, then add them to the pan with the onion. Stir in the paprika, then add the roasted capsicum and cook for a few minutes until fragrant. Turn off the heat and add the lemon juice. Allow to cool slightly, then transfer the mixture to a food processor and blitz to form a paste. Season to taste with salt. Sterilise your jars (see page 188).

Spoon the harissa into the sterilised jars and seal. Store the unopened jars in the pantry for up to 1 year. Refrigerate after opening and use within 1 week.

1 kg (2 lb 3 oz/5–6) red capsicums (bell peppers)
60 g (2 oz) olive oil
2 medium red onions, roughly chopped
45 g (1½ oz) garlic cloves, roughly chopped
2 long red chillies, seeded and roughly chopped
2 teaspoons coriander seeds
2 teaspoons cumin seeds
2 teaspoons fennel seeds
1 tablespoon smoked paprika
juice of ½ lemon
fine salt, to taste

TOMATO KASUNDI

FILLS 4 × 350 ML (12 FL OZ) JARS

This is an Indian spiced tomato relish that I use with many dishes. I love it on a brioche bun with egg and bacon for breakfast (page 61) – nothing like a bit of spice to get the day going. It's also great as an accompaniment to many savoury bakes, and with dal and rice.

———

10 long red chillies, roughly chopped (remove the seeds for a milder relish)

10 garlic cloves, roughly chopped

30 g (1 oz) fresh ginger, roughly chopped

150 g (5½ oz) olive oil

2 teaspoons black mustard seeds

2 tablespoons cumin seeds

180 g (6½ oz) apple-cider vinegar

1 kg (2 lb 3 oz) very ripe tomatoes, diced

130 g (4½ oz) coconut sugar

2 teaspoons ground turmeric

6 g (⅕ oz/1 teaspoon) fine salt

Put the chilli, garlic and ginger in a food processor and blitz to form a coarse paste.

Heat the olive oil in a heavy-based saucepan over a low–medium heat. Add the chilli paste and cook, stirring occasionally, for about 5 minutes, or until softened and lightly coloured.

Lightly crush the mustard and cumin seeds using a mortar and pestle, then add them to the pan. Cook for 2–3 minutes until fragrant. Add the vinegar, tomato, sugar, turmeric and salt and continue to cook over a medium–low heat for about 1 hour, or until the mixture has thickened. At this point, the oil will have risen to the top. Sterilise your jars while the relish cools (see page 188).

Pour the kasundi into the sterilised jars and seal. It is ready to eat straight away but do try to give it at least 1 week to mature. Store the unopened jars in the pantry for up to 1 year. Refrigerate after opening and use within 1 month.

Pictured on page 207.

FERMENTED LIME PICKLE

FILLS 4 × 300 ML (10 FL OZ) JARS

This pickle is an essential component of an Indian banquet, but will also make a meal of simple dal and rice. With two slow fermentation stages, this recipe takes six weeks from start to finish. We like to make it in large batches in winter when limes are abundant, so we have a jar in the fridge at all times. It also makes a great gift for any curry-loving mates.

Asafoetida is the dried gum of a variety of giant fennel. It has a strong pungent smell that really adds to this pickle. That same pungency can contaminate other spices it's stored alongside, so make sure you keep it in an airtight container. Asafoetida is great for people who can't eat onion and garlic, as it adds a similar depth of flavour to dishes.

I use a flat-ended rolling pin to muddle the limes during the first ferment, to soften the skins, or use a pestle if you have one. You'll need a large jar with a wide opening – wide enough to get your chosen muddling stick well in there.

Top and tail the limes. Cut each lime into eight wedges lengthways, then cut each length in half and put them in a large bowl. Combine the salt, turmeric and vinegar in a separate bowl and mix to make a slurry. Pour the slurry over the limes, then toss with your hands to ensure it is well distributed.

Put the limes in a large jar with a wide opening, cover with clean muslin (cheesecloth) or a tea towel (dish towel) and secure. Set aside for 4 weeks, muddling the limes for a minute or two every day to soften the skins. The sour smell of the citrus will start to become more pungent as it ferments.

Once the skins have softened, prepare the second ferment. Combine and finely grind all the spices using a mortar and pestle or spice grinder. Warm the olive oil in a small saucepan over a low heat. Stir in the spices, then remove the pan from the heat and set aside to infuse for 10 minutes.

Combine the water, coconut sugar and vinegar in a separate small saucepan over a medium heat. Cook for a few minutes, stirring until the sugar is dissolved. Slowly pour the sugar mixture into the spice-infused oil, whisking as you go. Set aside to cool, then pour it into the jar with the limes and mix well. Use a spatula to scrape down the side of the jar, ensuring that all the limes and spices are contained within the liquid. Cover once more with clean muslin or a tea towel. Keep the limes in the jar for another 2 weeks, stirring daily.

Sterilise your jars (see page 188). Spoon the lime pickle into the jars and seal. Store the unopened jars in the pantry for up to 1 year. Refrigerate after opening and use within 6 months.

FIRST FERMENT
500 g (1 lb 2 oz) unwaxed limes
60 g (2 oz/2½ tablespoons) fine salt
1 tablespoon ground turmeric
30 g (1 oz/1½ tablespoons) apple-cider vinegar

SECOND FERMENT
2 tablespoons brown mustard seeds
1 tablespoon fenugreek seeds
1 teaspoon asafoetida
1 teaspoon coriander seeds
1½ teaspoons cumin seeds
1 teaspoon Kashmiri chilli powder
50 g (1¾ oz/2½ tablespoons) olive oil
150 g (5½ oz) water
130 g (4½ oz) coconut sugar
20 g (¾ oz/1 tablespoon) apple-cider vinegar

CARAMELISED ONIONS

FILLS 2 × 250 ML (8½ FL OZ) JARS

I always have caramelised onions on hand. They are so tasty and can really boost the flavour of just about anything. I add them to pizza, pasta, quiche, galettes and sandwiches.

Use a heavy-based frying pan to slowly cook the onions over a low heat, scraping the bottom of the pan with a wooden spoon to prevent them sticking. Caramelise the onions to a light golden colour, just enough to draw out all the sugars and flavour. I aim for a light colour here so they won't burn when used in baking later on.

———

50 g (1¾ oz) unsalted butter
40 g (1½ oz/2 tablespoons) olive oil
1 kg (2 lb 3 oz) onions, thinly sliced
2 garlic cloves, thinly sliced
1 fresh bay leaf
5 g (⅛ oz) flaky sea salt
1 teaspoon freshly ground black pepper
1 tablespoon chopped thyme

Melt the butter and olive oil in a large heavy-based frying pan over a medium heat. Add the onion, garlic, bay leaf, salt and pepper and cook with the lid on, stirring occasionally, for 10–12 minutes to soften the onion and release the juices. The salt will help to draw the juices out.

Take the lid off and reduce the heat to medium–low. Cook, stirring occasionally, for a further 45 minutes to slowly caramelise the onions. The mixture will dry out and appear thick and glossy once ready. Stir in the thyme and taste for seasoning.

Store the caramelised onion for 1 week in the fridge. For longer storage, pour into sterilised jars (see page 188) and seal. Store the unopened jars in the pantry for up to 6 months.

NASTURTIUM CAPERS

FILLS 1 × 300 ML (10 FL OZ) JAR

We love nasturtiums in the garden for their abundance of flowers and foliage. They provide green cover on our garden fences and are a great companion plant for our vegetables. Throughout summer we use the leaves and flowers in salads and to make nasturtium butter, and in early autumn we rummage through the leaves looking for the seed pods to make capers.

The seed pods grow under the leaves in clusters of three. Make sure you pick young seeds that are still a little soft; once they get hard and yellow they are no good. Once pickled, you can use nasturtium capers the same way you'd use real capers. They're great chopped into salads, stir-fries, pasta sauces or dressings. A little goes a long way.

Go through the nasturtium seeds and remove any bits of dried flower, then rinse them to remove any dirt. Put them in a wide-mouthed heatproof jar, around 500 ml (17 fl oz) capacity.

Bring the water and salt to the boil in a small saucepan, stirring to dissolve the salt, then pour the hot brine over the seed pods. Put a cup in the top of the jar to ensure the seeds are completely submerged. Leave at room temperature for 3 days.

Drain the seeds and rinse to remove the excess salt, then put them in a sterilised 300 ml (10 fl oz) jar (page 188), or divide among several smaller jars. Bring the vinegar, sugar, bay leaves and thyme to a simmer in a small saucepan, stirring to dissolve the sugar, then pour the liquor over the seeds, including the bay and thyme. Seal the jar and turn upside down to create a vacuum.

Store the unopened jar in the pantry for up to 12 months. Refrigerate after opening and use within 3 months.

Pictured on page 208, centre.

150 g (5½ oz) nasturtium
   seed pods
500 g (1 lb 2 oz) water
60 g (2 oz/2½ tablespoons)
   fine salt
250 g (9 oz) white-wine vinegar
1 tablespoon raw (demerara)
   sugar
2 fresh bay leaves
4 thyme sprigs

WHOLEGRAIN MUSTARD

FILLS 2 × 300 ML (10 FL OZ) JARS

This wholegrain mustard is so straightforward to make. The ingredients are easy to find and the result packs more punch than anything you can buy in a jar. You can also tailor it, swapping out the dark ale for other liquids such as wine or water, or varying the herbs used. Brown mustard seeds are hotter than yellow, so if you like your mustard hot use more brown seeds. For a milder version, use more yellow seeds.

———

100 g (3½ oz) yellow mustard seeds
100 g (3½ oz) brown mustard seeds
80 g (2¾ oz) dark ale
240 g (8½ oz) apple-cider vinegar
60 g (2 oz) honey
20 g (¾ oz) flaky sea salt
1 teaspoon chopped thyme

Combine the yellow and brown mustard seeds. Use a spice grinder or mortar and pestle to grind 130 g (4½ oz) of the seeds into a fine powder. Combine the mustard powder with the remaining whole seeds in a medium bowl. Bring the ale to the boil in a small saucepan, then pour it over the mustard.

In a separate bowl, mix the vinegar, honey and salt until well combined, then whisk this into the mustard mixture. Transfer to a container and put in the fridge to mature for 3–4 weeks. After a week or so, give it a mix with a spoon to evenly distribute the mixture.

Once the mustard mixture is mature, add the thyme and stir it through thoroughly. Spoon into sterilised jars (see page 188). Store the unopened jars in the pantry for 12 months. The mustard matures in flavour the longer you keep it. Refrigerate after opening and use within 6 months.

Pictured on page 208, right.

CHILLI AND FENNEL SAUERKRAUT

FILLS 2 × 500 ML (17 FL OZ) JARS

If you want to get into lacto-fermentation and support good gut health, this is a great place to start. Cabbage releases a lot of water when mixed with salt, creating its own brine; it's an easy process and a hugely satisfying transformation to witness.

Lacto-fermentation occurs when you add salt to vegetables and then leave them out at room temperature for a period of time. The salt destroys harmful bacteria but preserves healthy *Lactobacillus* bacteria as the vegetables degrade. For best results, the quantity of salt used should be between 1.5 and 2.5% of the total prepared vegetable weight.

Traditional sauerkraut is made with caraway seeds, but I like to use chilli to give it more punch. There is nothing better than having a jar of sauerkraut in the fridge to add to a sandwich or cheese toastie.

Remove the stem from the cabbage, then shred the leaves into thin strips. Weigh the shredded cabbage and then calculate 2% of the weight; this is the exact weight for your salt.

Put the cabbage in a large bowl and add the salt. Use your hands to massage the salt into the cabbage for about 10 minutes. The cabbage will release its liquid to create your brine, so you must persist even when your arms get tired.

Add the fennel seeds and chilli and mix them through. Pack the cabbage into sterilised jars (see page 188), pressing down so it's tightly packed. Pour in the released liquid, ensuring it covers the cabbage – any cabbage not covered will spoil. If you don't have enough juice, add water to cover. Use a clean cabbage leaf and a sterilised weight on top of the pressed cabbage to help keep it submerged, and ensure you leave some room at the top of the jar for expansion during fermentation.

Seal the jars and leave to ferment at room temperature. After 3 days, remove the lid and push the cabbage down to compress it further, ensuring it's still covered with liquid. Leave it for another 2–4 days, depending on the weather. It will ferment faster in a warmer environment; a total of 5 days would be fine in summer, and up to 7 days in winter. After this initial fermentation, store the sauerkraut in the fridge to slow down the process. It is now ready to eat. The sauerkraut will last for several months in the fridge, developing a stronger flavour the longer it's stored.

1 green cabbage (approx. 1 kg/ 2 lb 3 oz)
approx. 20 g (¾ oz) flaky sea salt (2% of the weight of shredded cabbage)
2 teaspoons fennel seeds, lightly toasted
½ teaspoon chilli flakes

INDEX

A
all-purpose flour 14
almonds, Cauliflower and almond cheese pie 179
anchovies, Tomato and anchovy spelt galettes 97
apples
Brown sauce 198
Caramelised onion and apple chutney 200
asparagus
Asparagus, ham and cheese bostocks 116–17
Pea, asparagus and sour cream quiche 107
Potato, asparagus and gribiche tartes fines 120–1

B
bacon
Bacon and egg breakfast buns 61
Bacon and onion quiche 78–9
Rabbit, bacon and white bean pie 162
bakers (strong or bread) flour 14–15
Béchamel sauce 116–17, 179
beef
Gran's traditional Cornish pasty tarts 152
Steak and stilton pasties 86–7
Steak and Vegemite pie 109
Beetroot and shallot tarte tatin 156–7
black pudding, Pear and black pudding breakfast galettes 62–3
blind baking quiche and tart shells 18
blue cheese
Pumpkin and blue cheese galettes 168
Steak and stilton pasties 86–7
bocconcini, Ratatouille and bocconcini pie 106
bread flour 14–15
brioche dough 51–3
Asparagus, ham and cheese bostocks 116–17
Bacon and egg breakfast buns 61
Brown sauce 198
Buckwheat English muffins 66–7

buns, Bacon and egg breakfast buns 61
butter 16
vegan 46
Butter chicken pie 180

C
cabbage
Chilli and fennel sauerkraut 212
Root wellington 165–7
capers, Nasturtium capers 210
capsicums
Chorizo, red capsicum and manchego quiche 124–5
Harissa 204
Caramelised onions 209
Cauliflower and almond cheese pie 179
Celeriac, kale and hazelnut muffins 75
cheddar
Béchamel sauce 179
Cheese and onion pasties 91
Kimchi and cheddar puff pastry tarts 64
Spring onion and cheddar scones 72–3
cheese
Asparagus, ham and cheese bostocks 116–17
Cheese and onion pasties 91
Chorizo, red capsicum and manchego quiche 124–5
Greens, feta and ricotta hand pies 89
Paprika, cayenne and rosemary cheese straws 122
Pumpkin and blue cheese galettes 168
Ratatouille and bocconcini pie 106
Steak and stilton pasties 86–7
Zucchini, goat's cheese and rosemary loaf 133
see also cheddar; gruyère
chicken
Butter chicken pie 180
Chicken, sweet corn and basil pie 90
Thai green curry sausage rolls 178
chillies
Chilli and fennel sauerkraut 212
Habanero and mango hot sauce 203
Chorizo, red capsicum and manchego quiche 124–5

Choux pastry 44–5
Onion and gruyère gougères 141
chutney, Caramelised onion and apple chutney 200
corn *see* sweet corn
crackers, Rye sourdough crackers 127
cream 16
curry
Indian vegetable curry pie 181
Thai green curry sausage rolls 178

D
digital scales 12
dough scraper 12

E
egg wash 15
eggs 15
Bacon and egg breakfast buns 61
Pear and black pudding breakfast galettes 62–3
electric stand mixer 12
equipment 12

F
family pies 22
fan-forced ovens 12
fennel
Chilli and fennel sauerkraut 212
Smoked trout, fennel and nasturtium caper quiche 100
Fermented lime pickle 206
feta, Greens, feta and ricotta hand pies 89
fish
Fish pie 154–5
Smoked trout, fennel and nasturtium caper quiche 100
Tomato and anchovy spelt galettes 97
flaky pastry
gluten-free 22, 48–50
vegan 22, 46–7
Flaky shortcrust pastry 18, 22, 36–7
Bacon and onion quiche 78–9
Chorizo, red capsicum and manchego quiche 124–5
Mushroom, red onion and tarragon quiche 102–3
Pea, asparagus and sour cream quiche 107
Smoked trout, fennel and nasturtium caper quiche 100

wholemeal variation 36
whole rye variation 36
flour and grain 14–15
focaccia, Olive, rosemary and sea
    salt focaccia 143–5

G
galettes
    Pear and black pudding
        breakfast galettes 62–3
    Pumpkin and blue cheese
        galettes 168
    Tomato and anchovy spelt
        galettes 97
Gluten-free flaky pastry 22,
    48–50
    Pickled mushroom and
        macadamia tarts 92–3
    Potato, asparagus and gribiche
        tartes fines 120–1
gougères, Onion and gruyère
    gougères 141
Gran's traditional Cornish pasty
    tarts 152
Green tomato and tarragon relish
    199
Greens, feta and ricotta hand pies
    89
gruyère
    Asparagus, ham and cheese
        bostocks 116–17
    Béchamel sauce 116–17
    Ham and cheese palmiers 70–1
    Nettle and gruyère muffins 76
    Onion and gruyère gougères
        141

H
Habanero and mango hot sauce
    203
ham
    Asparagus, ham and cheese
        bostocks 116–17
    Ham and cheese palmiers 70–1
Harissa 204
    Moroccan wallaby and harissa
        sausage rolls 170
Hot water pastry 42–3
    Pork pies 137–8

I
Indian vegetable curry pie 181
individual pies 22–3
ingredients 14–17
intuition, using your 21

J
Jelly stock 137

K
kale, Celeriac, kale and hazelnut
    muffins 75
kangaroo
    Kangaroo, mushroom and ale
        pie 184
    Kangaroo, sweet potato, prune
        and preserved lemon pie 185
ketchup
    Pumpkin ketchup 185
    Tomato ketchup 184
Kimchi and cheddar puff pastry
    tarts 64

L
lamb
    Lamb shoulder, rosemary and
        barley pie 163
    Persian lamb sausage rolls 171
Lard shortcrust pastry 22, 38–9
    Gran's traditional Cornish pasty
        tarts 152
    Steak and stilton pasties 86–7
    wholemeal variation 38
limes, Fermented lime pickle 206
loaves
    Sweet corn and sour cream loaf
        135
    Zucchini, goat's cheese and
        rosemary loaf 133

M
Macadamia cream 92
manchego, Chorizo, red capsicum
    and manchego quiche 124–5
mangoes, Habanero and mango
    hot sauce 203
measurements 14
measuring tape 12
meat 16–17
Moroccan wallaby and harissa
    sausage rolls 170
muffins
    Buckwheat English muffins 66–7
    Celeriac, kale and hazelnut
        muffins 75
    Nettle and gruyère muffins 76
mushrooms
    Kangaroo, mushroom and ale
        pie 184
    Mushroom, red onion and
        tarragon quiche 102–3
    Mushroom, rye and preserved
        lemon pithiviers 160–1
    Pickled mushroom and
        macadamia tarts 92–3
    Root Wellington 165–7
mustard, Wholegrain mustard 211

N
Nasturtium capers 210
Nettle and gruyère muffins 76

O
Olive, rosemary and sea salt
    focaccia 143–5
onions
    Caramelised onion and apple
        chutney 200
    Caramelised onions 209
    Cheese and onion pasties 91
    Mushroom, red onion and
        tarragon quiche 102–3
    Onion and gruyère gougères
        141
    Pork, sage and onion sausage
        rolls 94
oven temperature 14
ovens
    fan-forced 12
    preheating 20

P
palmiers, Ham and cheese
    palmiers 70–1
pantry 188–213
Paprika, cayenne and rosemary
    cheese straws 122
pasties
    Cheese and onion pasties 91
    Gran's traditional Cornish pasty
        tarts 152
    Steak and stilton pasties 86–7
pastry 28
    brioche 51–3
    choux 44–5
    flaky shortcrust 18, 22, 36–7
    gluten-free flaky 48–50
    hot water 42–3
    lard shortcrust 22, 38–9
    puff 22, 32–4
    savoury shortcrust 22, 40–1
    vegan flaky 22, 46–7
    wrapping 20
pastry brush 12
pastry cutters 12
pastry scraps 20
    Sausages in scraps 136
Pea, asparagus and sour cream
    quiche 107
Pear and black pudding breakfast
    galettes 62–3
Persian lamb sausage rolls 171
Pickled mushroom and
    macadamia tarts 92–3
pickles, Fermented lime pickle
    206

pie dishes 12
pies
  assembling 22–3
  baking 23
  Butter chicken pie 180
  Cauliflower and almond cheese
    pie 179
  Chicken, sweet corn and basil
    pie 90
  family or pot 22
  Fish pie 154–5
  Gran's traditional Cornish pasty
    tarts 152
  Greens, feta and ricotta hand
    pies 89
  Indian vegetable curry pie 181
  individual 22–3
  Kangaroo, mushroom and ale
    pie 184
  Kangaroo, sweet potato, prune
    and preserved lemon pie 185
  Lamb shoulder, rosemary and
    barley pie 163
  Pork pies 137–8
  Rabbit and wild rice pie 176
  Rabbit, bacon and white bean
    pie 162
  Ratatouille and bocconcini pie
    106
  Steak and Vegemite pie 109
pithiviers, Mushroom, rye and
  preserved lemon pithiviers
  160–1
plain (all-purpose) flour 14
pork
  Pork, miso and soybean
    sausage rolls 174–5
  Pork pies 137–8
  Pork, sage and onion sausage
    rolls 94
portable digital timer 12
pot pies 22
Potato, asparagus and gribiche
  tartes fines 120–1
preheating ovens 20
Preserved lemons 192
  Kangaroo, sweet potato, prune
    and preserved lemon pie 185
  Mushroom, rye and preserved
    lemon pithiviers 160–1
Puff pastry 32–4
  Beetroot and shallot tarte tatin
    156–7
  Fish pie 154–5
  Greens, feta and ricotta hand
    pies 89
  Ham and cheese palmiers 70–1

Kimchi and cheddar puff pastry
  tarts 64
laminating 32
Moroccan wallaby and harissa
  sausage rolls 170
Paprika, cayenne and rosemary
  cheese straws 122
Persian lamb sausage rolls 171
Pork, miso and soybean
  sausage rolls 174–5
Pork, sage and onion sausage
  rolls 94
Quinoa and sweet potato
  sausage rolls 98–9
Root Wellington 165–7
Thai green curry sausage rolls
  178
whole rye variation 34
wholemeal variation 32
pumpkin
  Pumpkin and blue cheese
    galettes 168
  Pumpkin ketchup 195
  Pumpkin purée 128
  Pumpkin scones 128–9

Q
quiches
  Bacon and onion quiche
    78–9
  blind baking 18
  Chorizo, red capsicum and
    manchego quiche 124–5
  Mushroom, red onion and
    tarragon quiche 102–3
  Pea, asparagus and sour cream
    quiche 107
  Smoked trout, fennel and
    nasturtium caper quiche
    100
  Zucchini, spring onion and milk
    kefir quiche 132
Quinoa and sweet potato sausage
  rolls 98–9

R
rabbit
  Rabbit and wild rice pie 176
  Rabbit, bacon and white bean
    pie 162
Ratatouille and bocconcini pie
  106
red onions
  Brown sauce 198
  Caramelised onion and apple
    chutney 200
  Mushroom, red onion and
    tarragon quiche 102–3

relish
  Green tomato and tarragon
    relish 199
  Tomato kasundi 205
ricotta, Greens, feta and ricotta
  hand pies 89
roasted vegetables, Root
  wellington 165–7
rolling out dough 18
rolling pin 12
Root wellington 165–7
ruler 12
rye flaky shortcrust pastry 36
  Pear and black pudding
    breakfast galettes 62–3
rye flour
  Rye sourdough crackers 127
  Rye, walnut and anise myrtle
    scones 131
  Zucchini, goat's cheese and
    rosemary loaf 133
rye puff pastry 34
  Mushroom, rye and preserved
    lemon pithiviers 160–1

S
salt 16
sauces
  Béchamel sauce 116–17, 179
  Brown sauce 198
  Habanero and mango hot sauce
    203
  Sauce gribiche 120
  see also ketchup
sauerkraut, Chilli and fennel
  sauerkraut 212
sausage rolls
  Moroccan wallaby and harissa
    sausage rolls 170
  Persian lamb sausage rolls 171
  Pork, miso and soybean
    sausage rolls 174–5
  Pork, sage and onion sausage
    rolls 94
  Quinoa and sweet potato
    sausage rolls 98–9
  Thai green curry sausage rolls
    178
Sausages in scraps 136
Savoury shortcrust pastry 22, 40–1
scones
  Pumpkin scones 128–9
  Rye, walnut and anise myrtle
    scones 131
  Spring onion and cheddar
    scones 72–3
scraps for snacks 20

shallots, Beetroot and shallot tarte tatin 156–7

shortcrust pastry
    flaky 18, 22, 36–7
    lard 22, 38–9
    savoury 22, 40–1
Smoked trout, fennel and nasturtium caper quiche 100
sourdough starter 18–19
soybeans, Pork, miso and soybean sausage rolls 174–5
spelt flaky shortcrust pastry 36
    Tomato and anchovy spelt galettes 97
Spring onion and cheddar scones 72–3
Steak and stilton pasties 86–7
Steak and Vegemite pie 109
stilton, Steak and stilton pasties 86–7
strong flour 14–15
sweet corn
    Chicken, sweet corn and basil pie 90
    Sweet corn and sour cream loaf 135
sweet potatoes
    Kangaroo, sweet potato, prune and preserved lemon pie 185
    Quinoa and sweet potato sausage rolls 98–9

T
tarte tatin, Beetroot and shallot tarte tatin 156–7
tarts
    Beetroot and shallot tarte tatin 156–7
    blind baking 18
    Gran's traditional Cornish pasty tarts 152
    Kimchi and cheddar puff pastry tarts 64
    Pickled mushroom and macadamia tarts 92–3
    Potato, asparagus and gribiche tartes fines 120–1
techniques 18–19
Thai green curry sausage rolls 178
time 20
tomatoes
    Green tomato and tarragon relish 199
    Tomato and anchovy spelt galettes 97
    Tomato kasundi 205
    Tomato ketchup 194

V
Vegan butter 46
Vegan flaky pastry 22, 46–7
vegetables
    Indian vegetable curry pie 181
    Root wellington 165–7

W
wallaby, Moroccan wallaby and harissa sausage rolls 170
walnuts, Rye, walnut and anise myrtle scones 131
waste pastry 20
white beans, Rabbit, bacon and white bean pie 162
wholegrain flour 15
Wholegrain mustard 211
wholemeal flaky shortcrust pastry 36
    Zucchini, spring onion and milk kefir quiche 132
wholemeal lard shortcrust pastry 38
    Cheese and onion pasties 91
wholemeal puff pastry 32
wild rice, Rabbit and wild rice pie 176
wrapping pastry 20

Z
zucchini
    Zucchini, goat's cheese and rosemary loaf 133
    Zucchini, spring onion and milk kefir quiche 132

ABOUT THE AUTHORS

Michael James is a chef and baker who grew up in Penzance, West Cornwall, before moving to London, where he met Pippa over the pass at two-Michelin-starred restaurant Pied à Terre. They moved to Australia in 2004 and opened Tivoli Road Bakery in 2013. After garnering a loyal following for their bakery in Melbourne and beyond, and writing their first book together, *The Tivoli Road Baker*, Michael and Pippa sold the business to focus on life – and new opportunities. Together they are committed to sustainability and remain active members of Melbourne's baking, grain growing and milling community. In 2019, Michael set up the bakery at Alla Wolf Tasker's Dairy Flat Farm in Daylesford. He consults internationally and runs regular baking classes.

Follow @michaeljamesbakes and share your bakes #alldaybaking.

ACKNOWLEDGEMENTS

It has taken less than a year to make this book, and it was mostly created in the midst of the global COVID-19 pandemic, in lockdown, while home schooling. It has been a massive effort, so I want to thank all involved for their hard work, passion and dedication to make *All Day Baking* what it is. A book is all about collaboration, from start to finish.

I am grateful to everyone at Hardie Grant for giving me the opportunity to write another book and share these recipes. Many influences over the years – people and places – have informed and helped shape the book you are holding today.

Pippa James: Thank you for everything you do and have done in bringing all this together. It was a real challenge in such a short amount of time, but we did it, and I hope Clover can enjoy these recipes in years to come.

Geoff Smith: Thank you for taking care of Clover during lockdown so that this book could be made, and for testing some of the recipes.

Jane Willson: You are simply awesome to work with – a shame we had to do most of it via Zoom this time. The highlight of 2020 was making it out of lockdown just in time to do the shoot with you all in Daylesford. Thank you for believing in this from the start, I am so happy we got to do it all over again together!

Anna Collett: You got it from the start – so organised and thorough, and you kept it all ticking along when time was short. Cracking the whip and making sure the masks were on, it was a real pleasure working with you. A massive thank you for everything you did to bring this book together.

Dan Lepard: Thank you for checking in and for all the help, inspiration, hints and tips over the years.

Bonnie Ohara of Alchemy Bread: Thank you for the initial idea for a savoury (or savory) baking book and for help along the way.

Thank you to all the testers: Malissa Gough, Rebecca Rose, Claire Portek, Emily Wheeler, Justine Kajtar, Mik Halse, Julian Smith, Abbie Couper, Ally Akbarzadeh, Ana Caicedo, Zoe Greenwood, Ainslie Lubbock, Miriam Mosing, Dani Sunario, Michael Allen, Katie Ridsdale, Roslyn Grundy, Pamela Anderson, Isabel White, Nicola Roberts and Tina Smith.

Paul and Mark Jewell: Thank you for the inspiration through our pasty chats. I hope you enjoy these ones.

Clover: Thank you for being patient during home school and the lockdown while this book was being tested, written and shot at home.

Ella Cooper: It was great to work with you again, thank you for your help and precision during the shoot.

Andy Warren and Mietta Yans and the design team: Thank you for putting this all together, truly a wonderful job.

Kim Rowney: Thank you so much for being the most thorough editor, for all the questions that needed answers and for making sense of it all.

Lisa Cohen and Lee Blaylock: What a duo – the shoot went so smoothly and it was a welcome relief straight after lockdown. You created and captured the most beautiful photos.

Thank you to Troy and Chris at Meatsmith for all the meat for the photoshoot, and to Andrew at Small Batch Roastery for the use of your kitchen during the shoot.

Thank you to Sarah Owens, Justin Gellatly, Nat Paull, Chad Robertson, Chris Bianco, Helen Goh, Maggie Beer, Dan Hunter, Vanessa Kimbell and Edd Kimber for your beautiful and well considered words, and to Tom Aikens for the thoughtful foreword, and for taking me in as a raw cook and teaching me about cooking and baking at Pied à Terre all those years ago.

To Grandad: Thank you for all your hard work and all you did when I was growing up in Cornwall; none of this would be remotely possible without you. And Gran: Thank you for the initial baking lessons on the ironing board making all those pasty tarts … Miss you both.

Published in 2021 by Hardie Grant Books,
an imprint of Hardie Grant Publishing

Hardie Grant Books (Melbourne)
Building 1, 658 Church Street
Richmond, Victoria 3121

Hardie Grant Books (London)
5th & 6th Floors
52–54 Southwark Street
London SE1 1UN

hardiegrantbooks.com

Hardie Grant acknowledges the Traditional Owners of the country on which we work, the Wurundjeri
people of the Kulin nation and the Gadigal people of the Eora nation, and recognises their continuing
connection to the land, waters and culture. We pay our respects to their Elders past, present and emerging.

 A catalogue record for this
book is available from the
National Library of Australia

All Day Baking
ISBN 978 1 74379 699 3

10 9 8 7 6 5 4 3 2 1

Publishing Director: Jane Willson
Project Editor: Anna Collett
Editor: Kim Rowney
Design Manager: Mietta Yans
Designer: Andy Warren
Photographer: Lisa Cohen
Stylist: Lee Blaylock
Home Economist: Ella Cooper
Production Manager: Todd Rechner

Printed in China by Leo Paper Products LTD.
Colour reproduction by Splitting Image Colour Studio

I have been known to join the queue for Michael James' delicious food, and while I delight in his beautiful cakes and sweet treats, I marvel at his exquisite savoury baking: perfect pastry, on-point seasoning and interesting, but never gratuitous, flavours. In *All Day Baking*, Michael and Pippa have given us a collection of irresistible pies and pasties, homely scones and quiches, gorgeous galettes and tarts. And of course, those famous sausage rolls. Practical tips and friendly guidance ensure our efforts are rewarded, and a wonderful section on ketchups, relishes and chutneys tempt us even more to get (savoury!) baking. My only apprehension is that, with this book, I really do want to bake all day!

HELEN GOH, baker, author

I met Michael and Pippa years back at a grain gathering at the bread lab at Washington State University. What struck me first was their sincere passion for the foundation of all good things bread and pastry. This was beautifully represented at their world-renowned Tivoli Road Bakery in Melbourne. In their first book, *The Tivoli Road Baker*, Michael's full arsenal was on display. In this second book, he and Pippa give us the feeling and flavour of home, a focused all-day collection of savoury pies and pastry pulling from Michael's roots in Cornwall, England, kissed with time and a professional journey well spent.

CHRIS BIANCO, Pizzeria Bianco, author